Here's the Pitch

Here's the Pitch

How to Pitch Your Business to Anyone, Get Funded, and Win Clients

Martin Soorjoo

WILEY

John Wiley & Sons, Inc.

Published by John Wiley & Sons, Inc., Hoboken, New Jersey.
Published simultaneously in Canada.

For general information on our other products and services or for technical support,
please contact our Customer Care Department within the United States at (800)
762-2974, outside the United States at (317) 572-3993 or fax (317) 572-4002.

Wiley publishes in a variety of print and electronic formats and by print-on-demand.
Some material included with standard print versions of this book may not be
included in e-books or in print-on-demand. If this book refers to media such as a
CD or DVD that is not included in the version you purchased, you may download
this material at http://booksupport.wiley.com. For more information about Wiley
products, visit www.wiley.com.

Library of Congress Cataloging-in-Publication Data:

Soorjoo, Martin,1967–
    Heres the pitch : how to pitch your business to anyone, get funded, and win clients /
Martin Soorjoo.
        p.   cm.
    Includes bibliographical references.
    ISBN 978-1-118-13752-9 (cloth); ISBN 978-1-118- 22536-3 (ebk);
ISBN 978-1-118-23884-4 (ebk); ISBN 978-1-118-26343-3 (ebk)
        1. Business presentations.   2. Entrepreneurship.   3. Success in business.
    I. Title.
HF5718.22.S735   2012
658.4'52—dc23   2011043889

Printed in the United States of America

10 9 8 7 6 5 4 3 2 1

To my mother and father
for being the greatest
parents any son
could hope for.

Contents

Acknowledgments

This book is a collaborative effort that would not have come about but for the inspiration, support, input, feedback, and patience of family, friends, colleagues, and the team at John Wiley & Sons, Inc.

To my editor, Dan Ambrosio at Wiley, for first suggesting I write *Here's the Pitch* and for always being on the end of the phone. To my production editor, Lauren Freestone, for her excellent detective work.

To my mother, Jennifer, for her consistent support on multiple fronts.

To my wife, Margo, for putting up with me ruining our summer, but willing to still provide feedback and suggestions.

To my colleague, Jamie, at the Investor Pitch Clinic for his constructive feedback.

To Symon Drake-Brockman, Managing Partner at Pemberton Capital Advisors, for his mentorship, friendship, and providing me with my first insights into the mind of a seasoned investor.

To Kate for never hesitating to give me the bottom line.

And to the late Robert Davies, founding CEO of the Prince of Wales's International Business Leaders Forum, for his mentorship, friendship, and insights into the minds of Fortune 500 companies.

To San Francisco's Radio Alice for providing the background music which always makes burning the midnight oil a more enjoyable experience.

And last, to the hero entrepreneurs for whom this book is intended. Your optimism, vision, and courage continually inspire me.

INTRODUCTION

Life's a Pitch

"The only reason to give a speech is to change the world."
—John F. Kennedy

Former Chief Evangelist of Apple and entrepreneur supremo Guy Kawasaki tapped into the driving force of entrepreneurs when he named his blog "How to Change the World." Although money and success are prized, when entrepreneurs talk with passion about their product or service, they talk in terms of how it will help people or change lives.

It is passion and vision that enable entrepreneurs to make great sacrifices and take risks that transform their dream to reality. For many entrepreneurs, there is a point when the pitch becomes the opportunity to take the dream to the next level. So often, however, those same qualities that make achieving great things possible fail to take shape or appear during the pitch.

Those Who *Aspire* Must *Inspire*

Throughout history, great speeches have moved people and nations to take action and bring about change. Leaders have understood the power of a well-crafted speech, whether Abraham Lincoln's Gettysburg Address or Martin Luther King Jr.'s "I Have a Dream" speech, to inspire its audience. The late Steve Jobs was a master at inspiring people through his annual Macworld presentations, connecting with his audience and taking them on an exciting, unpredictable journey.

Yet although history shows us that you can only move people to take action by reaching both their hearts and minds, the vast majority of unsuccessful pitches are data dumps that reach neither. Instead, more often than not, they induce "Death by PowerPoint."

It is not enough for a pitch to simply inform. It must also engage and inspire. To achieve the desired impact, a pitch must, among other things, combine conversation, storytelling, and sales. Facts are never enough, and *efficiency* should not be confused with *effectiveness*.

Pitching in a Tough Climate

The collapse of the financial markets in 2008 has placed the entrepreneur center stage. The loss of jobs and job security has led to people of all ages, from all walks of life, aspiring to become entrepreneurs. Discussion is frequent in the media about whether entrepreneurship and innovation offer the best way out of the recession. An emerging theme of "hero" entrepreneurs was recognized by U.S. President Barack Obama in 2010, when he declared November 19 National Entrepreneurs' Day.

As the new generation of entrepreneurs is discovering, however, surviving and succeeding as an entrepreneur is more challenging than ever. According to the U.S. Small Business Association (SBA), at least 50 percent of start-ups fail within the first five years. Of those that continue, many barely survive.

Lack of capital is one of the primary reasons that new businesses fail. The collapse of the financial markets has meant that banks have stopped lending to small businesses and that investors are wary of start-ups.

This grim picture is reinforced by research that indicates that when it comes to pitching to investors, entrepreneurs have a 1 in 300 chance of success. On the sales front, companies have less money to spend, which has meant that winning a big sales contract is tougher than ever.

Information Overload

To add to the entrepreneur's challenges, time-strapped investors and corporate executives are distracted to an unprecedented degree by e-mails, texts, and social media. Old, overused pitch techniques, such as trial closings, rapport building, and inoculating against objections, are no longer sufficient to compete with increasingly limited attention spans.

Pitch to Win

Now more than ever, there is an urgent need to bring the power of communication and persuasion back to pitching. The understanding of emotions and psychology that has enabled speakers to inspire and motivate audiences for centuries must be readily embraced and utilized, alongside exciting findings from neuroscience about how the brain works.

During my 15 years as a successful attorney, I came to realize that the lawyers who consistently won did not always have the strongest cases, but they did always have the best trial skills. They knew how to successfully pitch to both judge and jury.

During my eight years of working with and coaching entrepreneurs and start-ups, I have seen a similar pattern. Entrepreneurs get funded and win new business even if their ideas, teams, and abilities to execute are not as strong as their counterparts'.

This means that, every day, entrepreneurs who should succeed fail, simply because they don't know how to pitch. This skill deficiency is compounded by the fact that to have any hope of getting a start-up off the ground, an entrepreneur needs to work around the clock and fill many roles. Consequently, very little time is left for developing pitching skills or preparing pitches. Too often entrepreneurs only begin to realize their importance after endless investor or sales pitch rejections.

Great Pitchers Are Made, Not Born

There's an often-repeated myth that you're either born a great pitcher or you're not. This myth simply provides a justification for not preparing properly and an excuse for why pitches fail. World-class communicators are often described as naturals. The truth is that these so-called naturals put in days, and sometimes weeks, of preparation and use an array of proven strategies and techniques to consistently win over their audiences.

Time and time again I have witnessed entrepreneurs with little or no experience develop into pitch superstars. Nearly 25 years as a professional pitcher and coach has proven to me, beyond a shadow of a doubt, that great pitchers are made, not born.

In this book, you will learn the same powerful strategies and techniques used by some of the world's greatest presenters, strategies and techniques that we teach our clients at the Investor Pitch Clinic and that I've personally used to raise millions of dollars from some of the toughest investors in the world and win sales pitches worth more than $70 million.

As you begin to develop pitch skills that mesmerize and motivate, you'll discover a new ability to get funded, win new business, and attract media coverage.

Everything You Need to Know about Pitching

This book is divided into four parts.

In Part I, you'll discover the fundamental pillars of pitching. You'll gain an understanding of the psychology of the pitch, including the key drivers of decision making and how you can create favorable power dynamics.

The greatest presenters of our time consistently use the same delivery strategies and techniques to spellbind their audiences. They know how to use their body language and vocal delivery for maximum impact and how to quickly capture and hold their audience's attention. Here, you will learn exactly what these techniques and strategies are and how to quickly master them.

Since we lived in caves, people have used the power of storytelling to inspire and educate others. You will learn what story elements work and how to incorporate them into your pitch.

Finally, the Q&A session is often the most challenging part of a pitch. When you know how to handle tough questions, you'll understand their potential to increase the effectiveness of your pitch. This part will show you how to make Q&A sessions work to your advantage so that you begin to welcome, rather than fear, them.

In Part II, I focus on the different forms that a pitch can take. I'll show you how to create quick, attention-grabbing high-concept pitches and elevator pitches that are essential in today's fast-paced world. As many entrepreneurs have discovered, shorter pitches are harder to develop and deliver than longer pitches.

Advances in technology and the ever-increasing popularity of social media has led to the rise of the twitpitch, e-pitch, virtual pitch, and video pitch. Pitching through these media, without the benefit of your physical presence or voice, requires a different approach, which I will teach you.

Every entrepreneur needs pitch documents, usually an executive summary and pitch deck. Most, however, are so badly created that they remain unread or deleted by the reader. Additionally, there are fundamental misunderstandings as to what documents are most effective for the different stages of the pitch process. Providing the wrong document at the wrong stage can damage, rather than enhance, your pitch.

I'll show you how to create an executive summary and pitch deck, which will grab your audience's attention within the first few seconds and inspire them to read to the end, as well as clarify what should be provided and when.

In Part III, I look at specific issues relating to the four audiences you're most likely to be pitching to, namely, investors, prospective clients, the public through crowdfunding, and the media. Different issues arise for each audience, and consequently different approaches and techniques are required.

One of the biggest challenges people face when pitching is overcoming fear and communicating confidence. In the United States, public speaking is the number one fear, and in the United Kingdom, it's number two (spiders are the number one fear). Advances in neuroscience have enabled us to understand both the causes and the cure.

In Part IV, I teach you how to prepare for your pitch by developing a winning mind-set.

You will learn how to rapidly eliminate fear and how to literally reprogram yourself so that you feel and communicate rock-solid confidence. I have taught these techniques to entrepreneurs, attorneys, and politicians for the past 10 years and have seen them work time and time again, sometimes in just an hour.

Finally, all successful presenters understand the importance of thorough preparation and the importance of investing time to do so. If you thought that Steve Jobs simply turned up and delivered jaw-dropping presentations without extensive preparation, you're very much mistaken. By putting in the time, great presenters create the illusion of being naturally great. This section will share with you preparation secrets that will enable you to deliver a winning pitch, time and time again.

Take Action

The ability to pitch is one of the most empowering, life-changing skills you can ever develop. Pitching is a skill that you can use in any area of your life that requires you to persuade people. This book will give you the ideas and the action plan to deliver high-impact pitches that will help you get funded and win clients, time and time again. Entrepreneurs know that ideas are easy to come by, but it's the taking action that counts. So let's start . . .

PART

I

The Mechanics of Pitching

1

The Power Dynamics of the Pitch

"Power is not only what you have but what the enemy thinks you have."

—Saul Alinsky, Author of *Rules for Radicals*

The power dynamics of a pitch is one of the most important determinants of success yet is rarely discussed or acknowledged. In life, all parties to all relationships have *some* power. The relative strengths, equal or unequal, stable or unstable, are continually subject to change.

In a pitch scenario, the dynamics are typically stacked in favor of the party the entrepreneur is pitching. The entrepreneur believes that he or she needs the funding or contract more than the investor or potential client needs him or her. As a consequence, the entrepreneur will often feel and communicate neediness, or worse, desperation.

This inequality of power is compounded by the fact that the investor or executive, typically Alpha, feels more powerful. Alpha has status within the organization and financial security and is usually *judging* the pitch on his or her home territory. Once this dynamic is established and allowed to continue, the entrepreneur's pitch is likely to fail or, at best, secure unfavorable terms. The good news is that you can take steps to increase your perceived and actual power.

Establish Favorable Dynamics at the Outset

On the basis that first impressions tend to set the scene, it's critical that you are proactive in creating favorable power dynamics at the point of first contact. This is important because a part of the brain called the adaptive unconscious (also referred to as the reptilian or limbic brain) causes people to make key judgments about you within the first few seconds of contact, long before you've reached the day of your pitch.

Psychologist Timothy D. Wilson describes the important role of the adaptive unconscious in his book *Strangers to Ourselves* when he states:

> The mind operates most efficiently by relegating a good deal of high-level, sophisticated thinking to the unconscious, just as a modern jetliner is able to fly on automatic pilot with little or no input from the human "conscious" pilot.

A study published in *Nature Neuroscience* took this understanding a stage further and concluded that our reptilian brain makes decisions before our conscious mind is aware of this. "Your decisions are strongly prepared by brain activity. By the time consciousness kicks in, most of the work has already been done," said study coauthor John-Dylan Haynes, a Max Planck Institute neuroscientist. In other words, investors or executives may have subconsciously written you off before they even knew it.

How Initial Decisions Are Made

The problem of decisions and judgments being made within the first few seconds is compounded by the fact that people make decisions on emotion and then justify them with fact. Although we may like to think of ourselves, first and foremost, as rational, cognitive human beings, consistent research has proved otherwise.

This fact of life applies equally to everyone, including lawyers, investors, and executives. The primacy of emotion and instinct in decision making is reflected in everyday business decisions. People decide to work with, or invest in, people they like or have a good feeling about but will point to the person's experience and qualifications as being the real reasons for doing so. People will buy from salespeople they like but then explain to family and friends that they really did need the purple Post-it storage box they just bought.

This isn't to say that nonemotional factors such as experience, qualifications, market size, or financial projections are irrelevant to the ultimate decision-making process. They are indeed relevant and important, just secondary. Secondary in the sense that if you don't start out by triggering the correct emotional responses in your audience, then even a strong business proposal, justified by hard data and numbers, will find itself pushing at a closed door.

Getting Past the Gatekeeper

Although many people are aware of the different roles of the left and right sides of the brain, few understand the differing roles of the reptilian brain and the new brain, which is the cerebral cortex. The reptilian brain is estimated to be between 300 million and 500 million years old, whereas the new brain is only 3 million to 4 million years old.

The primitive reptilian brain is where our emotions exist and is nonrational and nonreasoning. Its main purpose is our survival. By contrast, the new brain is the source of decision making and language. For the purposes of communicating and pitching, it's critical to understand that our message is filtered by the reptilian brain gatekeeper before it is deemed suitable for consideration by the recipient's new brain.

In *How the Brain Works*, Leslie A. Hart wrote, "Much evidence now indicates that the limbic area is the main switch in determining what sensory inputs will go to the neocortex and what decisions will be accepted from it."

What This Means for Your Pitch

The implications of the scientific research on how we process information and make decisions are significant for pitching. Put simply, if you do not send the right messages to your audience's reptilian brain at the earliest opportunity *and* continue to do so throughout your pitch, your chances of success are low. No matter how big your market or how solid your track record and financials, if you do not obtain reptilian brain approval, your message will not receive proper scrutiny by your audience's analytical brain.

The findings from the various scientific studies are consistent with my own experience and observations of pitches and court trials. It's always been clear to me that nonrational factors played an important part in the decision-making process, but it was only when I became familiar with the scientific research that I understood why.

Don't Convey Neediness

At the beginning of this chapter, I explained why it was vital that you don't come across as needy when pitching. There are two reasons for this. First, if someone appears desperate or needy, our reptilian brain becomes suspicious. Thoughts like, "Why does no one else want them?" or "How did they get into this desperate state?" will be generated. Alarm bells will start to ring, and your audience's reptilian brains will warn their new brains to steer clear of you.

Second, we tend to want and value that which we can't have or that which is difficult to obtain, and conversely we tend not to want or value that which is easy to get. This is a lesson many of us learned in high school— that frustrating problem of how the girl or boy you really wanted was always dating someone else or was just simply out of your reach.

Not long ago, I met with two friends who are seasoned angel investors (well connected, wealthy individuals who use their own money to invest). During dinner they discussed a Cloud services start-up pitch they had recently heard and were considering jointly investing in. What I found particularly interesting was the fact that their keenness to invest was significantly influenced by the knowledge that the founders of the start-up were in advanced discussions with other angel investors.

Now, although I am sure that neither of my friends would make an investment based solely on the fact that other investors were interested, it was equally clear to me that the fact that this start-up was being courted by other angels increased the chances of these founders being funded by my friends.

Be Desirable, Not Desperate

In *Influence: The Psychology of Persuasion*, Robert Cialdini, Regents' Professor Emeritus of Psychology and Marketing at Arizona State University, looked at this behavior through the prism of the *principle of scarcity*. Cialdini concludes that people assign more value to opportunities when they are less available.

The use of this principle for profit can be seen in high-pressure sales techniques. Examples include only a "limited number" now available or a "deadline" for an offer. When something becomes less accessible, whether due to quantity or time restrictions, the freedom to have such an item may be lost. According to psychological reactance theory, people respond to the loss of freedom by wanting to have it more. The trusty reptilian brain, in its effort to protect, will take steps to ensure that opportunities and freedoms are not lost.

This means that when you're pitching, it's vital that at no stage should you come across as desperate or needy. You want your audience to want you, not believe that you desperately need them. Ideally, you want to be perceived as the hard-to-get prize that everyone else wants.

This becomes easier once you remind yourself that investors need to invest in companies to make money and companies need to buy products and services from the right suppliers in order to operate, grow, and remain profitable. In other words, your audience is meeting with you because they believe you may have something they need. Your task is to convince them that they are correct.

Putting This Into Practice

If you're desperate for funding or a contract and feel you lack power in a relationship, your actions and words will convey this to the other party in a number of ways, including:

- Quickly agreeing to whatever time, date, and location the other party puts forward.
- Accepting whatever time the other party allows for the meeting; for example, you need 30 minutes to make your pitch and address FAQs but agree to the other party's proposal of 15 minutes.
- According the other party greater status. The other party, whether a venture capitalist (VC) or senior executive of a large multinational, may well have greater status than you; however, the minute you defer to that status, you give away your power.
- Allowing the other party to set the agenda even though it's your pitch.
- Agreeing to proceed with a meeting with subordinates in circumstances where you're told at the last minute that the key decision maker will no longer be attending.

There's a very fine line between maintaining your power and value and disrespecting the other party. You should always treat the other party with respect and as an equal. Wherever possible, however, in order to create and maintain a perception of your value, you should do the following:

- *Never immediately agree to a proposed time and place for a meeting.* You don't want to appear too available. Consider coming back with a counterproposal.

- *Always be ready to walk away from an unsatisfactory deal or offer of investment.* Simply making the commitment to yourself not to jump at the first offer and to being willing to walk away will increase your negotiating power and perceived value, as well as help in sending out a message of confidence. Obviously, if you are offered a great deal, take it!

- *Ask the other party to explain and elaborate on what they bring to the table.* If you are pitching investors, ask what else they bring in addition to capital (that is, connections and/or expertise).

- *If true,* subtly *let them know you are in meaningful discussions with their competition or other investors.* The key to doing this effectively is being subtle rather than obvious. During three years of pitching to Fortune 500 companies, I was left with the clear impression that nothing got a company's interest faster than knowing you were in discussions with their competition.

- *Never seek validation from the other party.* Do not ask whether they like your product or service or are impressed by your team's experience. You should know your own worth and should not seek their approval.

- *Finally, if you have been told you'll be meeting with the key decision maker and someone junior turns up at your meeting instead, you should normally refuse to proceed.* But offer to rearrange a time when the decision maker can meet. Aside from ensuring that you don't appear needy, you also avoid having the impact of your pitch on the decision maker watered down by their employee.

An extremely creative but equally disorganized entrepreneur that I worked with a few years ago (let's call him Ryan) had a highly effective system for persuading seasoned investors to pursue him, which in part involved establishing favorable power dynamics. Although uneducated, Ryan's deep understanding of human nature enabled him to raise more than $4 million from a number of angel investors without even knowing how to create an executive summary or PowerPoint presentation.

Ryan would frequently employ the following two techniques. First, when asked what he did for a living by his target investors, he would always make it sound as though he were already successful. Being careful never to mislead, Ryan focused on the positive and any successes that he had already achieved. He would also casually mention other investors, as well as others who were interested in his venture.

Second, Ryan would invariably leave the encounter at the point he was certain that his target's interest was at its peak. This seemed to be a variation on 'playing hard to get' which usually had the desired effect of his target making contact a few days later with a request that Ryan consider letting them invest.

Act as if

"If you want a quality, act as if you already had it."
—William James, Pioneering American
Psychologist, 1842–1910

If you think that you'll struggle to hide a perception of neediness during your pitch, then the technique of "acting as if" will help you convey a perception of confidence and success.

During the 2008 U.S. presidential campaign, political commentators observed that the then-Democratic presidential nominee, Barack Obama, often acted *as if* he were already president. He was viewed by many as having a presidential air and manner about him. This should come as no surprise as Obama once said that to inspire people, one must "always act confident."

William James, regarded by many as the father of American psychology, is credited with first introducing the concept of acting as if in his lecture "The Will to Believe," published in 1897. When you act as if you already have the quality or object you desire, a part of your brain called the reticular activation system (RAS) directs your behavior to narrow the gap between your present situation and the desired situation.

American artist, author, and metaphysician Florence Scovel Shinn wrote in *The Game of Life and How to Play It*,

> We have a wonderful illustration of this in the bible, relating to the three kings who were in the desert, without water for their men and horses. They consulted the prophet Elisha, who gave them this astonishing message: 'Thus saith the Lord—Ye shall not see wind, neither shall ye see rain, yet make this valley full of ditches.' Man must prepare for the thing he has asked for, when there isn't the slightest sign of it in sight.

To act as if, you need to get clarity on how a confident and successful entrepreneur behaves. You only need spend a few minutes on YouTube to see interviews with entrepreneurs who have successfully launched start-ups and made millions of dollars. Two great channels on YouTube that have plenty of useful videos are "This Week in Startups" and "This Week in Venture Capital."

Observe how the entrepreneurs communicate, how they dress, and how they think. Decide on which characteristics and behaviors represent success and confidence, and adopt them. As part of your pitch preparation, start acting with the confidence behaviors you observe, and you'll notice a change in how people treat and respond to you.

A Question of Judgment

By seeking to establish favorable power dynamics, you are simply taking control of a force that naturally exists throughout society, in every type of relationship, and indeed throughout the animal kingdom. When doing so, you should always act with integrity and modesty, rather than with deviousness and arrogance, not least because the other party's reptilian brain will defend against such behavior.

At the end of the day, you will have to decide how far you go when attempting to establish favorable power dynamics and your value. There will be those occasions when you stand to lose a valuable opportunity to pitch unless you agree to the other party's proposals. Most of the time, however, put your efforts in to establishing the right dynamics at the outset, and you'll ensure that you get your pitch off to a strong start and increase your chances of securing a great deal.

Takeaways

- Power dynamics are always present in every relationship.
- Establish favorable dynamics at the outset.
- Judgments about people are made in seconds.
- Don't be needy.
- Be desirable.
- Don't rush to agree to their terms.
- Act as if.

2

Stand and Deliver

"It is not what you say that matters but the manner in which you say it; there lies the secret of the ages."

—William Carlos Williams, American Poet, 1883–1963

Content matters. But in the way that great ideas fail because of poor execution, pitches often fail because of poor delivery. Delivery encompasses your body language as well as your vocal delivery. Research establishes that how you say is more important than what you say in your pitch. By using your body language and vocal delivery in the right way, you will more effectively engage your audience and persuade them to take the action you want.

This chapter will show you how to quickly and effectively use your body language and vocal delivery for maximum impact.

Energy

Presenters who use energy in their voice and body language to energize, excite, and motivate their audience. Energy is infectious and can inspire, raise spirits, and generate optimism during the toughest of times. Great examples of high-energy communicators include Oprah and successful entrepreneur and business leader Nido Qubein, who radiates warm positive energy that makes you smile. Peak performance coach Anthony Robbins is living, breathing, walking, talking energy. Robbins's high-energy performances motivate people to successfully walk across hot coals in their bare feet and make radical changes to their lives.

You cannot watch these communicators in action without being moved by their presenting style. Your audience wants to be energized and inspired, so make sure you inject energy into your performance.

Body Language

"What you do speaks so loud I can't hear what you say."
— Ralph Waldo Emerson

In landmark research, Professor Albert Mehrabian established that 55 percent of our messages are communicated through our physical behavior and appearance and 38 percent from the sound of our voice. Only 7 percent of what we actually say has any impact. In other words, a staggering 93 percent of your communication is transmitted nonverbally!

This means that when you give a presentation to an audience, 55 percent of your message is delivered through your body language. Visual sense dominates all of the senses. Yet when it comes to preparing a pitch, most people tend to ignore body language and instead focus on the content of their speech and their PowerPoint or Keynote presentation, if they are using one. This is one of the principal reasons why most people deliver bad pitches.

Given that most of your message is delivered through your body language, you would be well served spending most of your time perfecting your onstage gestures and movements.

The primacy of body language over verbal communication was illustrated in a study conducted by Professor

David McNeill, a psychologist, professor emeritus at the University of Chicago, and writer specializing in scientific research in psycholinguistics, particularly what gestures reveal about thought. In this study, participants were shown video recordings of various speakers telling a story. The speakers, however, used body language that was at odds with their verbal messages. When asked to tell the story, the participants found it easier to describe what they saw rather than what they heard.

> "The movements of expression reveal our thoughts and intentions more truly than our words, which can be falsified."
>
> —*Charles Darwin*

When pitching, you must use your body language to connect with your audience. The best pitches are those that create emotional impact, move people to take action, and leave them thinking about what you said for days afterward.

Connecting with people on an emotional level is important because people form opinions and make decisions based on their emotions. First, we listen to our emotional guidance system, then we justify with reasons. If the objective of your pitch is to persuade your audience and you don't make a connection, then your pitch is likely to fail.

When delivering your pitch, make sure you are constantly:

- connecting,
- engaging,

- projecting enthusiasm, and
- being expressive.

The following techniques are easy to implement but highly effective when used during a pitch:

- *Use hand gestures.* Although there are some people who advocate keeping your hand still at your sides, this old-fashioned, military style of communication is unnatural and has a negative effect on your overall communication impact. In *Hand and Mind*, McNeill explains that gestures do not simply form a part of what is said and meant, but they have an impact on thought itself.

    Your hands serve three purposes when pitching. First, hand gestures can bring a dull speech to life by infusing emotion and energy. Second, hands can illustrate and support verbal content. Third, you can use your hands to reach out to the audience.

- *Maintain an open posture.* Keep an open posture when pitching. Face your audience square on, and maintain sweeping eye contact. It is difficult to establish a connection when one party has physically turned away, or has closed themselves off, e.g., by folding their arms or has a barrier in front of them. This means never turning around to look at the screen and making sure there is no lectern or other physical obstacle between you and your audience.

- *Make eye contact.* It's extremely important that you make eye contact with people in the audience because this is one of the primary ways you connect with people. This is only possible, however, when you have prepared and rehearsed sufficiently so that you do not have to read from your slides.

Good eye contact equates with confidence and honesty and is therefore essential. It also has the benefit of enabling you to closely monitor how your audience is responding to your pitch. Move your gaze steadily around the room, and continually make eye contact with people. Make sure your eyes connect with your audience and communicate the emotions you want to convey.

- *Smile.* A simple smile is one of the most effective ways you can connect with people. Ronald Reagan was a great smiler and so are Bill Clinton and Oprah. A genuine smile conveys openness, warmth, and positive energy. Smile with your eyes and get your cheeks engaged. Our natural instinct is to like someone who is smiling, and all entrepreneurs need their audiences to like them.

Practice smiling in the mirror. You will be surprised to see that you are smiling less than you think you are. So in the beginning, until it becomes second nature, you may have to exaggerate your smiles when practicing.

Vocal Delivery

Your voice is the primary vehicle of your message. According to Mehrabian's research, our voice counts for 38 percent of our communication impact. As with body language, this key asset is usually overlooked when preparing for a pitch. A person's voice triggers immediate images. If you are speaking to someone on the phone whom you have never seen before, you immediately start to imagine what that person looks like once he or she starts talking. Similarly, an audience starts to make judgments based on your voice the moment you begin your pitch.

Use a Conversational Style

Given that one of the key objectives of your pitch is to engage your audience, you want to pitch as though you are having a conversation with them. Rehearsing so that you know your material inside out will make it much easier to communicate in a conversational style.

When pitching, focus on different members of the audience as you speak. Think in terms of having person-to-person conversations rather than delivering a one-way speech to the whole audience. When you make people think you are talking to them, you build connections and trigger empathy.

Slow Down

Nerves typically cause people to speak much faster during their pitch than they normally would. People often want to get through it as soon as possible. When you speak fast, you make it more difficult for your audience to digest the information you are providing. You also give away some of your authority because it can sound as though you are losing control. So slow it down.

Power of the Pause

Pausing is one of the most powerful and dramatic vocal techniques you can use during your pitch. Leaders from Winston Churchill to Barack Obama have used pauses to create impact in their speeches, focus attention on what has been said (or is about to be said), or to prepare the audience for a change in ideas. Steve Jobs would often add drama to his Macworld presentations by pausing at key moments.

President Obama used pausing with great effect at 02:45 in his inauguration address. He waited until the applause had died down and said, "My fellow citizens (3-second pause), I stand here today (3-second pause), humbled (1-second pause) by the task before us."

Recognition of the value of pausing is not limited to politicians. American comedian Jack Benny said, "When you are speaking, timing is not so much knowing when to speak, but knowing when to pause."

A pause of only 2 to 3 seconds has multiple benefits, including:

- Enabling you to breathe and maintain your composure.
- Slowing you down so that you sound more authoritative and in control.
- Enabling your audience to process the information.

- Giving you an opportunity to read the audience and assess how they are responding to your points.
- Helping you eliminate distracting nonwords such as *ums* and *ahs*.

Vary Your Vocal Delivery

One of the best ways to keep your audience's attention is to vary your vocal delivery throughout your pitch. You can vary your tone, pace, volume, and pitch. A dynamic voice with plenty of variation is energizing and can turn a sleep-inducing talk into a call-to-action speech. We all have different voices that we use for different purposes, whether it's a storytelling voice, a serious voice, or an enthusiastic voice.

Raising your pitch is equated with excitement and enthusiasm, so you might use this voice when you are talking about the large volume of orders you've received or the fact that your groundbreaking technology has just been granted a patent. In contrast, if you want to reassure your audience that you are able to lead your team and reinforce your authority, you would lower the volume and tone of your voice.

Takeaways

- How you say it is more important than what you say.
- Connect with your eyes.
- Use your body, hands, and vocal delivery to support and amplify your verbal message.
- Energy is essential.
- Pitch using a conversational style.

3

Engage and Inspire

"When you do the common things in life in an uncommon way, you will command the attention of the world."
—George Washington Carver

Most audiences lose interest in a pitch within minutes. If they do not suffer from Death by PowerPoint, they are murdered by monotony at the hands of a dull, lifeless speaker who inflicts on them a steady stream of facts and figures, thereby encouraging them to search out distractions.

To persuade an audience to take action, you need to secure their attention at the outset and retain it to the end of your pitch. This is difficult because the brain is easily bored and is continually subject to competing distractions and demands. This chapter reveals proven techniques and strategies that you can employ to keep your audience sitting on the edge of their seats, hanging on your every word, and talking about you long after you've gone.

Tell Them Timing

People have a need to be told how long they have to pay attention. Without clear information that the pitch will last a specific length of time, your audience is more likely to be distracted and unable to focus.

Make sure they know at the outset that your pitch will last for X minutes and then there will be a further Y minutes for Q&A. By doing this, you will not only have increased your audience's attention, but you will have communicated control, authority, and respect for their time.

Brevity Is Best

In terms of how long you should allow for your pitch, less is definitely more. The belief that the more information you provide in your pitch, the greater your chances of persuading your audience is fatally flawed. Throughout history, people have been inspired by the briefest of speeches. Abraham Lincoln's Gettysburg Address, regarded as one of the greatest speeches in American history, was only 272 words long and lasted 2 minutes.

Winston Churchill's famous "Blood, Toil, Tears and Sweat," speech, one of the finest calls to arms ever, given at the beginning of World War II when Hitler's armies were roaring across Europe, was only 688 words.

Early scientific research had concluded that people can maintain their attention for about 18 minutes before their minds begin to wander. More recently, however, John Medina, molecular biologist and author of *Brain Rules*, concluded, on the basis of peer-reviewed research, that after only 10 minutes, your audience's attention steadily drops. Medina states, "The brain seems to be making choices according to some stubborn timing patterns, undoubtedly influenced by both culture and gene."

The type of pitch may influence what would be an appropriate length. Typically, a venture capital pitch will be longer than a pitch to angel investors. As a general rule, you should keep your investor pitch to a maximum of 20 to 30 minutes. A sales pitch can be anything from 30 minutes to 1 hour. Whether it's 20 minutes or an hour, this is more than enough time to provide your audience with the information they need to make a decision.

Start Strong

"A bad beginning makes a bad ending."

—Euripides

Opening with an attention-grabbing, high-impact speech is one of the most effective ways to secure and retain your audience's attention. You can achieve this by using the following techniques:

- *Lead with your assets and achievements.* If you excite your audience at the outset with your strengths, whether sales and customers, validation by a reputable third party, patented technology, or a huge market, then they will want to hear more. This should be done within the first 60 to 90 seconds of your pitch.

- *Open with an interesting but relevant fact that your audience are unlikely to be aware of.* For example, if you were launching a new PC accessory that reduces the onset of repetitive strain injury (RSI) by 60 percent, you might tell your audience that more than 30 percent of PC users develop RSI at some point. That tells the audience there is a big market, it is relevant to them if they use a PC, and it demonstrates your knowledge of the sector.

- *Ask a rhetorical question, a question asked merely for effect with no expected answer.* For example, "Why are cigarettes sold in gas stations when smoking is prohibited there?" A relevant, thoughtful question is a very effective way of involving your audience in your pitch because it encourages the listener to think about the answer. The question should be rhetorical rather than direct because some people don't like being asked questions by the person pitching. So as soon as you've asked the question, follow up with the answer.

- *Use an analogy.* Dudley Field Malone said, "One good analogy is worth three hours' discussion."

If you are pitching a product or service that is new, complex, or difficult to explain, a well-thought-out analogy can help ensure that your audience understands within seconds rather than minutes.

A 2009 study conducted at the University of British Columbia showed advertisements for sports cars, massage chairs, and mountain vacations. Some ads used a features-and-benefits approach. Others used analogies, comparing the sports car to a first kiss and the massage chair to a hot tub after a hard day of skiing.

The study showed that audiences were approximately 50 percent more interested in products when the ads used analogies. This, the researchers concluded, was because the analogies generated positive memories and emotions that the subjects transferred onto the advertised product.

Keeping Your Audience's Attention

Even if you get your pitch off to a flying start and hook your audience's attention at the outset, you're still faced with the challenge of keeping their attention. The implications of Medina's findings should not be ignored. You have 10 minutes before you start to lose your audience. At this point, competing calls, texts, and e-mails will start to reclaim their influence.

One key to keeping your audience's attention is to be unpredictable and exciting. No audience wants to hear what they already know because if they know what's coming next, then why bother listening? According to Medina, "The brain doesn't pay attention to boring things, and I am as sick of boring presentations as you are."

Medina recommends introducing significant format changes every 10 minutes such as showing a demo or introducing a story (see Chapter 4). Steve Jobs was the master of keeping an audience's attention by constantly introducing new stimuli. Typically Jobs used demos, video clips, and even other speakers to keep his Macworld audiences engaged and excited.

Deliver an Unforgettable Moment

Standing out from the crowd and being memorable is one of the greatest challenges you face as a presenter. In most cases, your audience will have heard many pitches, and consequently, before you even open your mouth, they may be thinking, "We've heard it all before." Chances are they're right.

Great movies have one or more moments you never forget. Memorable movie scenes include Marilyn Monroe standing above a subway grating with her white dress blowing up in *The Seven Year Itch*; Clint Eastwood's advice to a bank robber, "You've got to ask yourself one question: do I feel lucky? Well, do ya punk?" in *Dirty Harry*; and Meg Ryan's "faking it" moment in *When Harry Met Sally.*

If you can deliver your audience an unforgettable moment, you will not only succeed in standing out and gaining their attention and engagement but will give them something to remember and discuss with others for a long time after. There are a number of ways you can achieve this, including:

1. *Using powerful visuals.* It is for good reason that it is often said that a picture is worth a thousand words. An image can instantly evoke an emotional response that words rarely can. Few will forget the famous video footage and photographs of a lone man in a white shirt standing in front of a column of tanks that were attempting to drive out protestors in Tiananmen Square in 1989. As the column approached an intersection, the unarmed man is shown standing in the center of the street, halting the tanks' progress. As the tank drivers attempted to go around him, the man moved into the tanks' path. He continued to stand defiantly in front of the tanks for some time, then climbed up onto the turret of the tank to speak to the soldiers inside. A photo of this scene was featured on the front page of almost every major newspaper across the world and captured the public's interest far more than any lengthy article could ever have done.

2. *Creating drama with your demo.* Steve Jobs did not simply present a demo. He presented dramatic moments that drove his audience wild. Possibly the

best example of this was the unveiling of the MacBook Air at Macworld 2008. Jobs introduced the MacBook by starting with a photo of an envelope on-screen and then telling the audience that the MacBook was "so thin it even fits inside one of those envelopes you see floating around the office." The audience roared with applause when Jobs then proceeded to open an envelope and pull out a MacBook.

Think in Threes

It has long been known that people understand and retain information better when it's presented in threes. It is no coincidence that there were three Stooges, Musketeers, and Bears (of Goldilocks fame). Great presenters know this and use the power of three throughout their presentations. Barack Obama often breaks his paragraphs into three sentences and will make three points.

You can use the power of three in your pitch in a number of ways, including driving home three key points that you want your audience to remember or by breaking your story into three parts.

Win With Words

"Words form the thread on which we string our experiences."
—Aldous Huxley

Words have the power to inspire or destroy, to make us happy or sad. Words are agents of change that can transform emotions, rather than vehicles that merely provide information. Used selectively in a pitch, the right words can instantly compel attention or trigger emotions.

Always use simple, clear language. Jargon and acronyms don't impress but may confuse your audience. Mission statements are great havens of jargon. The best presenters use simple, clear language that emotionally engages their audience.

Use inclusive language such as "So as *we* can see from the video." Using "we" rather than "you" helps remove distance and barriers between you and your audience.

Finally, use powerful words and phrases such as "We're *confident*" or "It's *clear* that *we will achieve* profitability by this quarter next year" rather than "We hope" or "We believe."

Takeaways

- Keep your pitch short and to the point. Less is always more.
- Start strong, opening with your assets and achievements.
- Be unpredictable.
- Create a memorable moment.
- Introduce changes in how you provide information during your pitch.
- Utilize the power of language.

4

The Power of Stories

"The problem is that nobody knows how to tell a story. And what's worse, nobody knows that they don't know how to tell a story."

—Don Valentine, Founding Partner, Sequoia Capital

In this chapter I will show you how to use the power and magic of story in your pitch so that you can inspire and motivate your audience to take the action you want them to.

Although entrepreneurs know they should use stories in their pitch, very few succeed in doing it effectively. When preparing a pitch, people typically focus on the facts and figures, then add some images, and finally might think about their delivery. This process usually occurs in a rush at the eleventh hour.

The end result is a data dump that neither inspires nor moves the audience to take action. Yet the very same information could be used to form the basis of a successful pitch, if only it were embedded in a compelling story. You will be more effective when you lead from the heart than when you lead from the head.

In part the facts-and-figures approach is driven by a mistaken belief that audiences, particularly investors, are only interested in the numbers. Everyone, including investors, prefers that their information be packaged in an inspirational human story, rather than as a dry data dump.

You can spend the time mastering a range of powerful delivery techniques, but delivery without a story is as effective as a courier company without transport. A well-crafted story is an effective delivery tool for your information.

Benefits of Using Stories

There are multiple reasons for using stories in your pitch:

- *People make decisions on emotion.* Stories move people to take action in a way data rarely does.

- *People love stories.* This began when we listened to stories as children and continues as we spend time going to the movies or reading fiction. Our love of stories means we are predisposed to storytellers.

- *Stories interpret facts and data.* They can even give meaning to numbers by providing scale and context.

- *Stories capture and keep attention.* Investors will turn into a quiet classroom of attentive young children instead of surly teenagers focusing on their smartphones, when listening to a good story. Your audience will continue to focus on what you say because they want to know what happens next.

- *Stories create empathy.* An empathetic audience is more likely to invest in your product/service or sign a contract with you.

- *Facts are forgotten, but stories are remembered and shared.*

The Story Creation Process

You must start with the story first and then add the facts and figures. Developing a story for your pitch is a right-brain creative process. This requires you to step back from the data and details and start to brainstorm.

To brainstorm effectively, you ideally want to get away from your normal working environment and go somewhere that inspires you. Alternatively, create your story after doing something that motivates you. This is necessary because it's difficult to inspire if you yourself are not feeling motivated.

Decide on Your Theme

All stories must have a theme running through them. The story theme is one of the primary emotional drivers that will motivate your audience to take action.

The following themes can be very effective for a pitch story:

- *The hero.* This can be you, your company, or your customer. Everyone loves a hero. A new company that is solving a big problem for ordinary people, for example, could position itself as a hero, as could a start-up offering a service at a substantially reduced price to the market leaders, thus making it affordable to the masses.

   You should also think about how you can make your audience the hero. Too often pitches are about me (the presenter) rather than you (the audience). If your audience invests in your company and consequently is able to bring a product to market that solves a genuine problem for people, then they are also heroes. Similarly, always look for ways that you can incorporate your audience into your story or make it relevant to them. By making them feel like a part of the story, they are more likely to want to support you.

- *Overcoming adversity and challenge.* This is an easy one because almost every entrepreneur faces a whole raft of challenges on a regular basis. Showing you have overcome serious challenges and are on the verge of success will instill confidence in an investor audience.

  Alternatively, you can show how your customers struggled with a challenge until they discovered your product.

- *David and Goliath.* This theme would be appropriate when your company (David) is entering an arena full of Goliaths with deep pockets but your solution is better. With your audience's support, David will be able to beat Goliath.

- *Your vision.* This can be a very powerful call to action if you can inspire your audience with your vision of how things will be when you bring your product to market.

  Grasshopper, the company that created a virtual phone system specifically for entrepreneurs, is a great example of a company that inspires its market. At the time of this writing, their "Entrepreneurs Can Change the World" video had more than 800,000 views on YouTube.

- *Your or your customer's story.* Personal stories bring authenticity into the room, and authenticity is an extremely powerful catalyst for action. A story of how a customer has used your product to solve his or her problem not only provides a theme but also validation.

Essential Ingredients for Your Story

Once you have determined theme, then you need to work out the central character. This can and probably should be you, your company, or your customer.

Look for opportunities to introduce drama in your story. This is one of the best ways to captivate attention. This should be easy because entrepreneurs usually have lots of drama in their lives.

Then you need to determine the single point of the story. Is it that your solution solves a big problem? It's important to never lose sight of the point of the story and remind the listener of it throughout your pitch. Similarly, your story must clearly define the benefit to your audience.

Is there a villain or antagonist? Having one of these characters present will always make a story more exciting. They could be the competition or a government department.

Think about how you can arouse curiosity or include surprise. A surprise twist or ending will increase your audience's engagement and connection with you. The more you can use your story to take the audience on a journey, the more effective your pitch.

It's important to note, however, that your story doesn't have to run whole of the pitch. It is woven into your pitch but doesn't replace it. A short story or fragment of a story may be enough to make your point and achieve your goal of engaging your audience.

Finally, introduce the contrasting theme of this is how things are but this is how they could be if your product or service is available.

Bringing Your Story to Life

How you deliver a story makes a difference in how it is received. Energy and measured passion will ensure your audience sticks with you to the end of your pitch. You don't want to sound as though you're delivering a bedtime story, so enthusiasm is essential.

Supporting images work well with stories rather than competing text on a presentation. An appropriate picture really is worth a thousand words. People will not be able to focus on listening to you if a slide loaded with text is competing for their attention.

Once you have worked out your story structure, then you can add the data and details. Facts and figures add credibility to a story and help transport it from the realm of fiction to fact.

The following will help bring your story to life:

- *A demo of your product.* Seeing really is believing when it comes to pitches, and a demo is a very effective way to make your pitch real. If you don't have a working demo, make sure you bring along a video or visual representation.

- *Rich, descriptive, sensory language.* Mark Twain said, "A powerful agent is the right word. Whenever we come upon one of those intensely right words . . . the resulting effect is physical as well as spiritual, and electrically prompt."

  Appeal to the eyes, ears, and heart of your audience, and you'll increase their understanding and attention. Words don't simply affect emotions; they create action. Inspirational leaders throughout history, from Abraham Lincoln and his Gettysburg Address to Martin Luther King Jr.'s "I Have a Dream" speech, have used the power of language to capture the hearts and minds of their audience.

- *Magical metaphors.* A metaphor is a tool for communicating a problem or solution to an audience. José Ortega y Gasset said, "The metaphor is perhaps one of man's most fruitful potentialities. Its efficacy verges on magic, and it seems a tool for creation which God forgot inside one of His creatures when He made him."

Jesus, Mohammed, Confucius, and Buddha all used metaphors to communicate with the people, as do modern-day leaders. During a 2010 fund-raiser in Manhattan, President Obama used several metaphors when referring to Republicans, including describing them as "bad drivers" who still want the car keys.

Although some entrepreneurs might describe the feeling of pitching to investors as "going into the lion's den," you should take the time to create one or two metaphors for your pitch to add impact, clarity, and connection.

And They All Lived Happily Ever After

Creating and using a story in your pitch is not difficult. Remember that you are always telling stories to your friends and family about what you experienced or saw.

When you do this, you are naturally engaging and persuasive. Think about how you tell stories to your family and friends, and make sure that you, the storyteller, is the person who does the pitch.

Takeaways

- Data dumps fail; stories succeed.
- Everyone loves stories, even investors.
- People make decisions with emotions first and they rationalize second.
- Stories give facts and data meaning.
- Facts are forgotten; stories are remembered and shared.
- Every story needs a theme.
- Bring your story to life.

5

Handling Questions

"Sometimes questions are more important than answers."
—Nancy Willard, American Poet and Writer

Things can be going great during your pitch until that moment when you come under fire in the form of challenging questions from your audience.

No matter how well you've prepared, there is a good chance that at least one question will make your heart sink and head spin. When that happens, the lights seem brighter, time seems to stop, and all eyes are focused on you.

Handle this question badly or alienate your audience, and it may all be over. At this point a nervous tick, defensiveness, inappropriate body language, and facial expressions all seem amplified.

It isn't possible to prepare for every question you may be asked, but this chapter will show you how to respond, even when asked the unexpected and the difficult.

Welcome Questions

Entrepreneurs can struggle when asked questions during a pitch because they perceive the questions to be a problem rather than an opportunity. Questions are an opportunity to prove your expertise, enhance your credibility, and provide further reasons for your audience to take the action you want them to.

You should never assume the purpose of the question reflects a concern about you or your start-up unless it's explicitly critical. There are always at least three possible reasons for questions.

First, the questioner seeks clarification of an issue you have covered or should be expected to know the answer to. When addressing your financial projections, you may tell your audience that you anticipate a 30 percent increase in sales next year. If you have not explained the basis for this assumption, you can expect someone in your audience to ask why you anticipate the increase.

Second, the questioner is kicking the tires and wants to know whether you and your product are robust. An investor audience may ask you for a detailed breakdown of the results of your beta testing (the last stage of testing a product). A potential corporate client may ask you how many complaints you have had about the product you are trying to sell them.

Third, the questioner disagrees with something you have said and wants to debate the issue. Financial projections are an area where investors nearly always disagree with an entrepreneur's often optimistic view and will want to challenge.

All of these questions indicate a level of interest and engagement from your audience and provide you with an opportunity to shine. If you assume the questions to be hostile, your body language, tone of voice, and facial expressions will naturally become defensive. This in turn will impact your chances of providing a response that reassures and persuades your audience, so it's essential that you start to welcome questions.

Handle Questions Like a Pro

Lawyers and politicians are great pitchers who are used to fielding difficult questions from judges, probing reporters, and angry members of the public. You may recognize some of the following techniques they use during media interviews.

Steady Hand

It's essential that an entrepreneur has a steady hand at all times during a pitch. Succeeding as an entrepreneur is, at times, as hard as surfing a tidal wave. The mark of a successful entrepreneur is one who can remain calm in the most difficult circumstances.

The moment you lose control of your emotions, you lose credibility. Your audience will forgive you for not knowing an answer, but they're unlikely to back an entrepreneur who falls to pieces because they don't know the answer.

So although you can't control what questions you're going to be asked, you can control how you respond. Whatever happens during your pitch, you must remain cool and calm from start to finish.

You can communicate your steady hand to your audience by not answering questions too quickly and controlling your body language (see Chapter 2). Taking time to reflect on the question and formulate your answer shows maturity and self-control and ensures that you provide a better response.

Focusing in on the Questioner

There will be times when you're asked questions that seem pointless or irrelevant. If your audience detects you think this and believes you don't respect them, then your ride will get rougher. Deal with this situation in the following way:

- Focus your attention on the person who asked the question. Make sure you are squarely facing and looking directly at him or her. Nod your head as the question is asked.

     The more the questioner thinks you are taking the point seriously, the more willing he or she will be to reciprocate, consider, and accept your answer. Seasoned pitchers know to respond to a turkey of a question by replying, "That's a great question."

     It's a very disarming tactic.

- When responding to the question, use the terms *you* or *your question*. This enables you to establish a connection, again making the questioner feel respected.

Buying Time

There may be times when you can't fire off an instant reply to a question you have been asked, but you know the answer is somewhere in the back of your mind. An effective technique for buying critical time is to repeat the first part of the question.

For example, if you're asked, "What is the anticipated year-one profit margin on the new product you are launching next quarter?"

Assuming this is something you know the answer to but need a couple of seconds to pull out, you can begin your answer by stating, "The anticipated profit margin for X is . . ."

There are two benefits to this technique. The first is that it buys you time to pull the answer from your memory or properly formulate your answer. The second benefit is that the act of focusing and repeating the question causes your brain to act like a heat-seeking missile looking for the information you need.

Why You Shouldn't Script Your Answers

For many entrepreneurs, part of their preparation involves creating a list of questions they expect to be asked and then drafting proposed responses.

Although there's great value in identifying in advance the key issues you are likely to be asked about, there's a potential downside to scripting your answers that can be quite damaging to your performance.

The problem arises when you wrongly perceive the question you've been asked as a question you have prepared the answer to. This can occur because you are so focused on delivering your carefully prepared answer for this particular issue that you have not noticed that it is the same issue but a different question.

This results in you giving the wrong answer, which may suggest to your audience that you're either being evasive or not listening properly. So when a person asks a question, give them your full attention and put your prepared answers out of your mind.

Never Gamble With a Guess

When asked a question, people tend to feel under pressure to provide an answer. This is normal. When asked a question during a pitch, you have to exercise control and make sure you know the correct answer.

If you don't know the answer, then don't guess! Simply say something like, "I don't have that information available right now but will come back to you within the next 24 hours."

Most people will respect that approach. If, however, you guess and are exposed as being wrong, you may be regarded as either being untruthful or incompetent.

Dealing With Direct Criticism

There may be times when you're in a pitch that you find yourself on the end of aggressive questioning. When this happens, it's important that you are able to step back and ask yourself, "What's really behind the question?" Don't be distracted by the questioner's tone or manner; instead focus on the information he or she requires.

If it's clear that he or she is being critical of you, then you need to deal with this in a way that addresses the concern without appearing defensive.

The use of a combination of paraphrasing and reframing techniques when faced with this type of situation is highly effective.

Paraphrasing involves restating a statement using a different form of words. Reframing is a communication and therapeutic technique used by practitioners of neuro-linguistic programming (NLP) that refers to giving another perspective or meaning to a situation or statement.

The following example illustrates these two techniques in action.

The chief executive officer (CEO) of a major automobile manufacturer is meeting with potential investors seeking to raise $1 billion to fund the development of a new eco vehicle at a time when they have just had to lay off 850 employees. A potential investor fires the following question at the CEO:

"We all know the automobile sector is going down the pan. And you have just had to make hundreds of employees redundant. So it doesn't make sense for you to be thinking of focusing on a new prototype vehicle when you already have enough on your plate."

Using some of the techniques covered earlier in this chapter (squarely facing and looking directly at the questioner while nodding), the CEO might respond something along these lines:

"That's a fair point. Making our organization leaner has meant that our business is now in a much stronger position. First, we are able to maintain our position as a market leader by taking advantage of the growing demand for greener vehicles. Second, we will be one of the first automobile manufacturers to benefit from the financial incentives that are being provided by the government to companies who invest in greener technologies."

By focusing on the key issue being raised by the potential investor and by using a combination of paraphrasing and reframing, it's possible to respond in a positive manner, highlighting future opportunities rather than difficult points in history.

Common Questions During Pitches

As stated previously, it is impossible to prepare for each and every question that you're likely to be asked, but it is always useful to think about the possibilities. After you have several pitches under your belt, you will begin to notice the same types of questions coming up time and time again.

Investor audiences, for example, are always interested in the *how* and *what* questions, such as:

- How will you stop established players in your market from copying and/or bettering your solution?
- What are your barriers to entry?
- How much money do you have in the bank today?
- How will you scale?
- What is the basis for your Q2 projections?
- How will you acquire customers?

Potential corporate clients may ask you during a sales pitch:

- Have you talked to our competition?
- How will you cope when you receive several large orders?
- Why should we buy from you and not from your competitor?
- How do we know you will be able to deliver when you have no track record?

An entrepreneur who is able to deal with difficult questions during a pitch will clearly be perceived as more credible than one who clams up or gives a bad answer. Practice using these techniques during your daily interactions with people, and you'll be better prepared for those times when you come under fire during a pitch.

Takeaways

- Questions are opportunities.
- Maintain a steady hand at all times.
- Don't script answers.
- Never gamble with a guess.
- Paraphrase and reframe rather than defend and offend.

Forms of Pitch

6

Attention-Grabbing Pitches

"Everything should be made as simple as possible, but no simpler."

—Albert Einstein

In today's time-crunched world it's essential that an entrepreneur is able to deliver a concise, attention-grabbing description of his or her business. More than ever, people are bombarded with information from every angle. In this era of fast pitching, investors have hundreds and hundreds of approaches from start-ups. By keeping it simple, you give yourself the chance to cut through and stand out. A high-concept pitch and elevator pitch are the most effective tools for achieving this objective.

Hail the High-Concept Pitch

Originating from the literary world, the high-concept pitch is the ultimate simple, distilled expression of your business proposition. It has the object of capturing your audience's attention (introducer or investor) and planting your proposition in their memory.

Hollywood has generated some memorable high-concept pitches. *Alien* was pitched to studio executives as "*Jaws* in space." Other notable examples include:

- YouTube—"Flickr for video"
- Crowdify—"Facebook for brands"
- LinkedIn—"Facebook for business"
- Cisco—"We network networks"

Why Keep It Simple

I practiced as a successful attorney for 15 years. One of the keys to winning the majority of my cases was keeping it simple. Although many other lawyers would confuse judges and juries with legal jargon and irrelevant technical data, I always tried to make my legal argument as simple as possible for the judge and jury.

The importance of simplicity was reinforced in my mind when I hired a leading advertising agency to create an ad campaign for a company I was advising. This ad agency's mantra was "brutal simplicity of thought," and it was clearly a key to their success.

The Multiple Benefits of a High-Concept Pitch

In addition to capturing the initial interest of an investor, a good high-concept pitch enables your customers to instantly understand your product or service and become advocates, spreading the word using your pitch. And if you are lucky enough to get positive media attention, you make it easier for them to communicate your business using the frame you want.

Crafting a Great High-Concept Pitch

It is far easier to make something sound complex and unappealing than it is to make it sound simple and sexy.

The process of coming up with a compelling high-concept pitch can take days of brainstorming. The effort is worth it.

Step back and decide what is it about your business proposition that is most likely to generate interests. Organize brainstorming sessions for you and your team, and get creative. As we saw with the *Alien* and YouTube examples, a common approach is to link your proposition to other successful ventures. Once you have come up with one or more draft high-concept pitches, run them by people who know nothing about your venture, and see how they respond.

A Picture Can Paint a Thousand Words

A high-concept can be expressed in words as a short sentence or as a visual. I once secured an agreement from the CFO of one of the world's top 50 companies to meet to discuss a $36 million deal on the basis of a single visual slide that had no words, just one picture. Clearly, not all business propositions can be expressed in this way.

Remember the Purpose of Your High-Concept Pitch

The purpose of a high-concept pitch is to generate interest. It's important, however, that your high-concept pitch does not intentionally mislead by deliberately creating a false impression. A great high-concept pitch is one that gets attention and still makes sense once the audience knows more about your venture.

Spend the time trying to get it right, and you will find that a well-crafted high-concept pitch is one of the most effective ways of getting that critical initial interest from would-be investors or clients.

The Elevator Pitch

The elevator pitch is one of the most useful tools an entrepreneur can have, yet it's also one of the most misunderstood and misused. In part, this is due to a flawed perception that its purpose is to secure a deal or investment, when in fact it's usually the first step on the path to achieving your goal.

The Purposes of an Elevator Pitch

As an entrepreneur, you will have multiple uses for elevator pitches, including:

- Getting the initial interest of an investor,
- Attracting the attention of a company you want to pitch your product or services to,
- Persuading a third party to provide an introduction to an investor or company,
- Starting a conversation with someone you want to develop a long-term business relationship with, and
- Generating media interest.

Despite the name, elevator pitches are rarely used in elevators but are popular in situations where entrepreneurs come into contact with investors or executives such as at conventions or networking events. They are also becoming increasingly popular at pitch events, where entrepreneurs are given a couple of minutes to pitch to a panel of investors.

Entrepreneurs will often scour the events looking for prey, armed with deadly pitches. Indeed, many an investor has complained about being pitched to while at the urinal! An elevator pitch is also useful, however, for those unplanned occasions when someone useful crosses your path and is interested in hearing about you and your company.

In today's fast-paced *e* and *i* world, investors and company executives are ferociously busy with endless competing demands for their attention. A well-crafted elevator pitch is an effective way of cutting through the noise and gaining interest without causing information overload. The aim of a good elevator pitch is to whet the appetite of your audience and leave them wanting more, not to give them indigestion!

Elevator Pitch Guidelines

To deliver a good elevator pitch, apply the following guidelines:

- *Keep it shorter than 2 minutes.* On average, people speak comfortably at 150 words per minute, so your pitch should typically be no more than 300 words.

- *Don't use acronyms and jargon.* Just because you're immersed in your industry and live the lingo doesn't mean your audience does. Given the limited time you have, you want the listener to understand every word.

- *Keep it simple.* Your audience's limited time and attention span mean they need the information packaged as simply and clearly as possible. Complex does not equal clever.

- *Keep it conceptual.* Although it is often said that the devil is in the details when it comes to your elevator pitch, you should focus on concepts and keep the discussion at a high level. Your elevator pitch is the opportunity to excite your listener with the big picture, so focus on concepts at this stage, and save the details for later.

- *Focus on the what, not the how.* A common mistake is to focus on operational and technical details. If your audience is interested in the what you're pitching, you will get an opportunity on an another occasion to discuss the how. If, however, they don't understand the what, there won't be a second chance.

- *Avoid hype.* The best way to tune your audience out is to start talking about your "world-leading, cutting-edge, game-changing" technology. Use solid facts and figures, and you'll keep your audience and your credibility.

- *Tailor your pitch.* One pitch does not fit all situations. A different audience will usually require a refinement of your pitch. If you're pitching your company to an investor, you would normally include some financials. If, however, you're pitching to the chief executive officer (CEO) of a company that you're hoping will become a customer, you would be more likely to focus on the benefits of your solution.

Delivery Matters

A common side effect of having to deliver an impromptu pitch in a relatively short space of time is a tendency to deliver the information at the speed of light in hard-sell mode. Don't! I frequently have to tell entrepreneurs trying their pitch out on me to stop and take a breath.

Despite its name, you want your elevator pitch to be a *conversation*, not a *presentation*. You need to speak in your natural communication style because this will be much easier to understand and easier on the ear. It also gives the listener the opportunity to engage with you and ask questions.

When you use a conversational style, you're able to observe how your audience is receiving your pitch and adapt or clarify any point if necessary.

Be Adaptable

Whatever type of pitch you're delivering, you need to be able to instantly adapt and respond to cues and questions from your audience. An engaged audience may not want to let you run the full course of your pitch and may ask you to elaborate on a specific issue such as who your target customer is.

This means you need to view each segment of your elevator pitch as free standing so that you can deal with topics out of sequence and expand and contract other parts as necessary. If you haven't properly prepared and practiced, being asked a question in the middle of your pitch can completely knock you off course.

Structure

When it comes to pitching, I prefer to talk in terms of an approach rather than hard and fast rules. This is because no two pitches are the same, and what works for one pitch may not always work for another. The same approach applies to structuring an elevator pitch. Although the following ingredients tend to remain the same, the order in which they are delivered can change.

- *Overview sentence.* In Chapter 7 I discuss the importance of including an overview paragraph at the beginning of your executive summary and pitch deck. The same applies to your elevator pitch.

  Make sure you start out summarizing your pitch in one sentence. For example, "I am the founder of Axiom, which has developed a new type of seat belt for child passengers in cars, which reduces the risk of injury by 50 percent if there is a collision."

  You'll see that the key components of your overview pitch are who you and your company are, what your solution and its benefits are, and finally who your target customer is. The components might be different with a different pitch. For example, if Microsoft was one of your customers, you would obviously want to mention this in your overview sentence.

  There are two benefits to starting with an overview. First, you have set the scene with the most compelling parts of your pitch and, as such, are more likely to keep your audience's attention for the duration. Second, if for any reason your pitch is cut short, you've already provided the most important information that your audience needs to hear and are best placed to follow up on another occasion.

- *The problem.* Here you concisely define the problem and explain who is suffering. You should explain why existing solutions are inadequate.

- *Your solution.* Here you provide more information about your solution. Explain the benefits and why it's better than existing solutions. Think benefits first, features second. For example, "Our app will automatically let people know you're running late to a meeting so you don't have to pull over when you're driving" rather than "Our app is compatible with 70 percent of smartphones."

- *The market.* This is important for an investor pitch rather than a sales pitch. Explain your total addressable market (TAM) and who your target customer is. Avoid the classic mistake of focusing on the whole market rather than your segment.

- *Traction.* Again, this is particularly important when pitching to investors and will help establish your credibility. To be taken seriously, you should show that you are making progress and have some achievements you can talk about. This can include customers and sales, obtaining a patent, or recruiting an experienced management team.

During a pitch to one of the world's largest oil companies, a senior executive said of our start-up,

"There's no question that you are a train going somewhere fast—the only question is whether we will be on it."

Pitching your ideas, hopes, and dreams is not going to get you anywhere in today's market. If you want action, pitch traction.

- *The team.* For many decision makers the team is as important as the solution. For some investors the team is the most important factor. Provide a concise description of your key management players and highlight relevant experience and achievements. If you have a big team you only need mention the important members, or alternatively you can summarize the team's total experience. For example, "Our management team has a combined experience of more than 75 years in the sports apparel industry."

- *The ask.* As the saying goes, "If you don't ask, you don't get." *You* need to let your audience know exactly what you want them to do. Rarely, if ever, will this be a request for investment or a contract. In most cases it will be a request for a meeting, call, or their agreement for you to send more information to them.

Takeaways

- Always make it simple.
- Making it simple takes time.
- Never use jargon.
- Always use structure.
- Always adapt.

7

The e-Pitch

The availability of low-cost, efficient web communications technology, coupled with the rise of social media, is leading to an increased use of virtual and Web 2.0 pitches. Although these newer forms of pitches will never be as effective as a face-to-face meeting, they clearly offer advantages in terms of time and cost savings. In this chapter we will look at the twitpitch, virtual pitch, video pitch and e-mail pitch.

The Twitpitch

With the number of people using social media increasing exponentially every year, it was inevitable that pitching would begin to cross over from the real to the virtual world. Although a social media pitch has limitations, it can play a valuable part in the overall pitching process, particularly at the outset.

Social media expert Stowe Boyd is credited with first coining the term *twitpitch* in 2008. Boyd was attending a Web 2.0 Expo and was attempting to schedule meetings with start-ups. He posted on his blog that he would not accept e-mail proposals, only twitpitches.

Boyd set out the following rules regarding twitpitches on his blog:

- All companies who would like to have a meeting with me, need to send me a Twittered description of the product. Yes, please Twitter it to me at www.twitter.com/stoweboyd. Yes, one tweet, 140 characters less the eleven used for "@stoweboyd".

- Optionally, send a supporting twitpitch with one link, and no other text. Could be to anything: website, video, press release, Rick Astley, etc.

- Then, twitter me one or more suggested times/place to meet at the event, using the times on the calendar, and a location in the conference building. I won't have time to visit your nearby hotel or offices.

Since then, the twitpitch has been used and defined in many different ways. In 2009 Richard Branson invited start-ups to twitpitch him for investment.

Investopedia defines twitpitch as:

> A slang term used to describe an overview of a product or service that is short enough to fit in the character limitations of the social networking website Twitter. A twitpitch is a variation of an elevator pitch, but with the constraint being the 140 character limit imposed by Twitter instead of the time spent in an elevator.

A twitpitch is sometimes referred to as an *escalator* pitch as opposed to an *elevator* pitch on the basis that it is short enough for someone to read and understand on an escalator ride. A twitpitch can be used for more than just the purpose of providing an overview of a product or service and can:

- Get the interest of investors.
- Get the interest of journalists. A number of journalists now specifically request that any story pitches be sent via Twitter.

- Provide a concise description of your product or service that your Twitter followers can share.

Creating an effective twitpitch takes time, and the same principles that apply to other forms of pitching equally apply to twitpitching, namely:

- *Do not twitpitch a stranger straight off the bat.* A cold twitpitch is unlikely to be warmly received. Focus on developing a relationship first, and once that is in place, then pitch. You can establish a relationship on Twitter by simply interacting with the other person without asking for something. You can share information they might be interested in or comment on a tweet they have shared.
- *Make it about them.* When crafting your twitpitch, put yourself in the other party's shoes, and think about what is likely to interest them. Apply the filter of what's in it for them to your twitpitch.
- *Recognize a twitpitch's limitations.* Twitpitches are more effective when viewed as interest-generating tools than as an explicit sales or investor pitch. The limitation of 140 characters makes it unlikely that you will be able to deliver a pitch that sells you in the best possible light, so why even try?

  Far better to aim to take your relationship either to a platform where you can have a more meaningful interaction such as e-mail, LinkedIn, Facebook, or the phone. At this point it will be easier to persuade the other party to meet, and at that stage you can deliver a full pitch. So think about an interesting hook that will likely stimulate curiosity. Make sure to include a link to your website or blog that will provide your target with more information.

- *Be persistent.* The nature of Twitter means that people will often miss your twitpitch. This is particularly likely if they have a large number of followers, as many investors do. Do not make the mistake that one entrepreneur did of twitpitching an investor more than 20 times in one week using the same pitch.

  The entrepreneur unwittingly rendered himself *persona non grata* and destroyed any chance of a pitch via any other channel receiving a positive response. Vary the content of your twitpitches, and if need be, try another communication channel. Not all people are receptive to being pitched to on Twitter or monitor the tweets and mentions by their followers.

- *Don't overpitch.* If you are pitching to your followers, this is key. First and foremost, Twitter is a social media platform, not an advertising platform. People will tolerate and respond to the occasional twitpitch but will ignore and even unfollow you if your tweets are one nonstop pitch. I recommend a ratio of one twitpitch to every four or five regular tweets.

- *Provide valuable content.* One of the most effective ways to get attention and attract buyers is to provide useful, relevant content. Some of it should be content-generated on other people's sites (e.g., from other bloggers). You would mention the post and

include a link. But some should be content you have
generated yourself that is available on your website
or blog. This way people will come to your site to
read the content, and you then have an opportunity
to pitch to them at that stage. To paraphrase kung fu
legend Bruce Lee, this could be described as "the art
of pitching without pitching" (*Enter the Dragon*).

- *Don't pitch as a direct message (DM)*. Some people
  regard this as intrusive and others rarely check their
  DMs. Your twitpitch should simply be a regular
  tweet that begins with the recipient's Twitter name.
  For example, "*@Johndavis—thanks for sharing your
  great post on valuation*."

The Virtual Pitch

The virtual pitch is the next best thing to a real pitch.
Using web meeting technology, you can have real-time
meetings with people halfway across the world without
the cost of travel or time. You can see and hear each other
and share and show presentations. So it's no surprise that
this form of technology is becoming increasingly popular
for pitches.

In 2010 Bain Capital Ventures, the venture capital
affiliate of the Boston-based private equity firm Bain
Capital, opened a virtual center for connecting entrepreneurs with experts and Bain principals or associates.

WebEx estimates that more than 12 million meetings take place every day. Additionally, there are now

more than 100 web presentation platforms. Although it
will be some time, if it ever happens, before the number of virtual pitches reaches the level of face-to-face
meetings, entrepreneurs need to make sure they develop
and hone their virtual pitch skills for the day when a
prospective client or investor asks to meet using a web-
based platform.

The Problem With Virtual Pitches

Before looking at how you maximize your virtual pitch
impact, it's important to acknowledge the shortcom-
ings of pitching this way so that you can take steps to
compensate. Virtual pitching combines two of people's
most common challenges—fear of public speaking and
fear of using technology—so, inevitably, problems arise.
Challenges include:

- A reduced ability to make a connection with your
  audience. Nothing competes with meeting in person
  to build a relationship.
- An inability to read the other party and gauge how
  he or she is responding to your pitch. This limits the
  presenter's ability to adapt the pitch based on visual
  cues from their audience, whether a confused expression or enthusiastic nodding.
- The audience being free to be distracted by their
  smartphone or other reading materials without the
  presenter's knowledge.
- A lack of interaction.

- The loss of your presentation's impact. Presenting via a single screen is not as impactful as pitching in person with the assistance of a visual presentation.

Making the Technology Work for You

Since their first introduction in the 1990s, web-based presentation platforms have consistently introduced new features that increase the interactive and dynamic nature of a web meeting. By making full use of these features and increasing audience engagement, you limit the scope for their attention to wander.

Features that you should consider using include:

- *Document sharing.* Rather than send your visual presentation in advance, the document-sharing feature enables you to share documents at appropriate points throughout the pitch. For example, when discussing financial projections, you could share your spreadsheet or graphs with your audience.

- *Application and desktop sharing.* With this feature you can share any application that sits on your computer. This is particularly useful for sales or investor pitches where you want your audience to experience using your demo or actual product. This is virtual pitch interaction at its finest.

- *Annotation tools.* These tools allow you to annotate your visual presentation during your pitch, for example, by highlighting a part of one of your slides. Because you are not there in person to keep your audience engaged, it's important to keep a level of activity throughout so your audience does not zone out from staring at a single slide for several minutes.

In terms of basic technology, you need the following:

- *A reliable web presentation platform.* Given that your pitch impact is already reduced by pitching virtually, do not compromise on the standard of provider that you go with. There are plenty of options to choose from, and the intense competition in this space has driven down the cost.

- *A good webcam.* Although webcams use up a lot of bandwidth, they are the best way of making a connection with your audience.

- *A fast broadband connection.* Virtual meetings are notorious for poor sound quality and frozen pictures. This is invariably due to a slow broadband connection, although in some cases can be caused by a slow PC. To avoid this, both you and the other party need fast connections.

- *Good audio.* Do not make the mistake of using your PC microphone. Either use a good-quality headset with voice-over Internet protocol (VoIP), which you can pick up for around $50, or a landline telephone, again with a headset. Do not use a cell phone because the quality varies throughout a call. The importance of using a headset is that it enables you to keep your hands free, which means you will present more effectively. It also leaves you free to operate your PC when you need to.

The Pitch

Most of the techniques and principles covered elsewhere in this book apply with equal force to virtual pitches. There are a number of steps you can take that help minimize your lack of presence and increase your audience's level of attention and engagement.

First, do not treat the virtual pitch as a data dump. You can and should still seek to inspire your audience through the use of the techniques discussed in Chapters 2 through 4, for example, story and surprise.

Second, do not revert to use of a text-heavy visual presentation. People cannot read text on-screen and listen to you at the same time, whether you are there in person or not. This problem is compounded by the fact that you will not be viewing your audience for most of your pitch, so you will not know whether they are listening to you or reading the screen.

The principles relating to presentation design outlined in Chapter 8 apply to virtual presentations. Primarily use high-quality images and very little text.

There is, however, one key difference. Because you are not physically present, there is less visual stimulus. This increases the probability of your audience being distracted or losing attention if they are left staring at the same slide for too long. One solution is to increase the number of slides you show. Every time you introduce a new slide, you will reset the audience's attention.

Third, use the annotation tools to highlight or draw attention to a particular aspect on the slide. This is usually most appropriate when showing charts or graphs.

The annotation activity on-screen helps keep the audience engaged.

Fourth, share documents and, if relevant, allow your audience to try out your demo or application through the document- and application-sharing features that most platforms offer.

Finally, alternate between yourself on webcam and your visual presentation. If you were presenting in person, your audience's attention would switch between you and your presentation, so by alternating on-screen you create a more realistic experience. Always begin your pitch by talking to your audience via your webcam so that you establish a connection at the outset. You can also increase the stimulus and variety by copresenting with another member of your team. You should, however, only do this if you would have done it in a face-to-face pitch. Request that your audience use a webcam because it can be disconcerting presenting to an audience you cannot see.

Using Your Webcam

When using your webcam, try not to move around too much because even slight movements appear amplified and exaggerated on-screen. In order to increase your ability to establish a connection with your audience, make sure you are looking them in the eye. Many webcams tell you exactly where to look to establish eye contact. Finally, be careful what you wear; stripes, whites, or bright colors can be very distracting on-screen. Choose a single plain color that isn't too bright.

Rehearsal and Preparation

Much of the advice contained in Chapter 14 is relevant to virtual pitches. In some respects, because a virtual pitch involves the use of an additional layer of technology, careful preparation is even more important.

Run several full rehearsals using the same equipment and web presentation platform that you will be using on the day of your real pitch. This has the benefit of ensuring you are familiar with the equipment and technology, as well as enabling you to identify any potential areas of concern such as poor audio quality.

In terms of feedback, pitch your rehearsals to a real audience of friends and colleagues, and video the pitch. Many of the leading web presentation platforms enable you to record everything that happens during your pitch such as audio, video, chat conversations, and notes. Most people are surprised to see and hear how badly they come across during their first virtual presentation, so practice and preparation are essential.

The Video Pitch

The video pitch is particularly popular with entrepreneurs looking for funding. Increasingly entrepreneurs are sending video pitches to venture capitalists and angels in place of a traditional executive summary or pitch deck. The problem is that most video pitches are poorly created and consequently miss the mark.

A common complaint from investors who receive video pitches is that the entrepreneur spends a few minutes staring into the camera, speaking in a monotone voice, and fails to show the product.

Many of the same principles that apply to virtual pitches apply to video pitches. The key difference is that there is no scope of interaction, which means that careful thought has to be put into securing the viewer's interest within the first few seconds and holding it for the duration of the video.

The following guidelines will help you gain the maximum benefit from your video pitch:

- *Keep it short.* View your video pitch as an elevator pitch. Its purpose is to generate interest and lead to a call or meeting. This means it should ideally be no longer than 2 to 3 minutes.

- *Start strong.* In the same way that you want to secure a reader's interest within the first one to two paragraphs, you want to try and secure the viewer's interest within the first 10 to 15 seconds. Remember, you will not be present if and when they view the video, so they will feel under no obligation to watch it to the end. Use an overview approach, and highlight your strengths within the first few seconds.

- *Script what you intend to say and have a clear flow.* Every second counts, so a tightly worded script will ensure that you don't wander or forget what you are going to say. If you rehearse a few times before the real recording, you won't need to read from the script. Use a flow similar to the elevator pitch flow, outlined in Chapter 6.

- *Show the viewer your product, demo, or prototype.* As with virtual pitches, start by talking directly to the camera, but quickly move to showing the viewer the product or service you are pitching.
- *Film with a plain or white background.* This ensures that the viewer's focus remains on you or your product.
- *Edit your video.* The one advantage of a video pitch over a virtual pitch is that you can edit any mistakes and reshoot.

E-mail Pitch

An e-mail pitch is one of the hardest ways to secure a meeting or call with an investor or prospective client, but it is also one that requires the least effort. Every week I hear of entrepreneurs who have managed to secure a meeting on the basis of an initial e-mail. It may have been their 35th e-mail (not to the same person!), but if you don't have a third-party introduction, it's worth the effort.

As with any pitch, you need to be realistic about what can be achieved and clear about your objectives. The objective of an e-mail pitch is to generate sufficient interest in the reader, so that they request more information. The following template has been used more than once to secure a call or meeting with an investor:

Hello [Name],
My name is [Name], and I am the founder/CEO of [Company].

We [have created/are launching/have launched] a product/service that does [Y].

We [summarize some of your key traction, for example, sales/customers].

You can read more about my company here [URL to company]. My profile is available here [link to a completed professional profile such as LinkedIn, not Twitter].

I am sure you are extremely busy but would greatly appreciate it if you took a moment to consider this information and look at our company.

If you would like to know more, I can send you our executive summary and/or pitch deck and would be happy to call or meet with you any time that you are available.

I'll follow up next week to check if you have had a chance to consider this e-mail.

Thanks, and I look forward to hearing from you.

Best,

[Name, Title, and Contact Details]

This template is short and polite, concisely summarizes the product or service, and offers the reader the opportunity for more information, either through clicking on the links or by requesting further documentation. Although the chances of succeeding this way are lower than with other types of pitches, it certainly should feature as part of an entrepreneur's overall pitch strategy.

Takeaways

- Set realistic objectives for your e-pitch.
- Build relationships first; pitch second.
- Virtual pitches require preparation and research.
- Make your virtual pitch interactive.
- Show; don't tell.

8

Pitch Materials

The Executive Summary and Pitch Deck

"Less is more."

—Ludwig Mies van der Rohe, Architect

The Executive Summary

In our fast-paced world, investors rarely read business plans, and clients are not interested in lengthy presentations. Even if you have a great elevator pitch, most investors will ask to see your executive summary before meeting you. It's your door opener and in many cases the first impression you give to the recipient. This means it is often the most important document in the pitch process.

Less Is More, but Not Easier

An executive summary should be a two- to three-page distillation of your business plan and no more. Given that the document is a summary, it logically follows that you should ideally create it *after* you have completed your business plan. It's difficult to summarize what you haven't written.

Although investors tend not to read lengthy business plans, it is still worth creating one because the process of building forces you to focus on many issues that are easily overlooked when you are running at full steam trying to launch your start-up. If you have a management team, you should involve them in the creation process, as your document will be addressing all major areas of your business.

Do not make the mistake, however, of assuming that because your executive summary is relatively short, it follows that it's easy to create. As a general rule, it's always more difficult to tell a story in a concise, effective manner than it is to tell it in the course of several pages or hours.

A famous exchange between Mark Twain and his publisher illustrates the point well. Twain's publisher contacted him, asking for a two-page short story in two days. Twain replied, "No can do 2 pages, two days. Can do 30 pages, two days. Need 30 days to do 2 pages."

People often underestimate how long the creation process takes. Being concise and clear is one of the hardest communication skills to master. Be prepared to set aside days, not hours, creating and perfecting your executive summary. Given that your opportunity to meet with an investor or potential client may turn to this document, you cannot spend too much time making sure you get it right.

Appearances Matter

Although substance is most important, appearances still matter when it comes to your pitch documentation. In the same way you wouldn't show up to your pitch looking scruffy, you should always make sure your documentation is well formatted and polished. You need both substance and style.

It's important that your executive summary be as easy to read as possible. You don't want to make the reader work hard to understand your content. A friend, who is a seasoned angel investor, once told me that if he struggles to read the first few paragraphs of an executive summary, he files it in the trash. His reasoning, he explained, is that if the entrepreneur cannot clearly communicate when trying to raise badly needed investment, then there is no hope of this person successfully pitching to clients once he has the money.

Contrary to popular but bad practice, your document shouldn't be crammed with graphics and pictures but should ideally:

- Be approximately two to three pages.
- Be created with size 10 to 12 font.
- Be single-spaced.
- Use subheadings.
- Use paragraphs.
- Use bullet points.

Content

Now that you know the basic guidelines for formatting an executive summary, we can look at what should be included.

Since the economic crash, investors are more risk averse than ever. It's important to avoid creating a document that reads like a shopping list of hopes and dreams. It should include a record of your relevant achievements with some concrete planning for the future. If you haven't already gained some traction with your start-up, you'll have an uphill struggle trying to get funded. Pitch traction if you want your reader to take action.

The remainder of this chapter suggests an order and list of contents for your executive summary. Chapter 9 provides greater detail on content. Ultimately, you'll need to decide what content you include, and this in part will depend on the nature of your business and its stage of development.

1. Introduction   Always lead with your strengths so as to create a good first impression and hook the reader from the outset. Your introductory paragraph should be two to four sentences long and provide an overview of your business. It should include:

- Your business name.
- Description of your product/service.
- The market you compete in.
- The need your product/service meets.
- The market demand.
- How your product will be or is being sold.

This is the most important paragraph of your executive summary. You need to generate enough interest so that the reader is motivated to read the remainder of the document. Remember, many investors are bombarded with pitches every day of the week, so you need to be clear, stand out, and hook them fast.

Although you want to inspire and excite the reader, you need to avoid using a hyped approach. For example, "Our company has developed a cutting-edge, world-leading social networking platform that will become the market leader within 12 months."

That sentence doesn't tell the reader anything meaningful about the business and suggests inexperience and naïveté. The key lies in presenting your strengths in a positive but accurate and factual manner. A more effective sentence might be, "Company X has created the first social networking platform for doctors, nurses, and other health professionals who struggle to develop and maintain friendships because of the long, unsociable hours they work."

2. Background and Milestones   In this section, expand upon the information in your introduction, providing some background and context. It's helpful to signpost in summary form, where you're proposing to take the business. For example, "In September 2012 we will launch our premium paid service and anticipate having 350,000 users 12 months later."

3. Product/Service Overview—Value Proposition   This is the reason your business exists. What's the pain that your product/service addresses? Explain who's suffering and how they're currently solving the problem. It's important that you don't make assertions that are unsupported either by common sense or hard data. It isn't enough that you passionately believe there is a problem and would buy your solution.

This section is also where you should address why current solutions are inadequate and how yours is better.

4. Market   How big is your market? You should deal with this topic in terms of both overall market size and segment growth. This will reassure the reader that you have

an in-depth understanding of the true market opportunity. Wherever possible, you should rely on recent data
and independent research to support your assertions and
cite the source, for example, Forrester.

Although every investor wants to hear that you have
a big market, you must be realistic with your assess-
ment, which means starting with your total addressable
market (TAM).

You can deal with the competition here or create
a separate section. Don't make the mistake of suggesting that you have no competitors (unless it is really true)
because this will undermine your credibility. If another
company is solving the same pain as you, albeit in a different way, they are competition. Competition is a good
thing—it suggests there is a real problem to be solved—as
long as there's space for you.

5. Target Customers   In this section you need to define
who your customers are and how they will use your
product/service. This applies whether you are a business-
to-business (B2B) or business-to-consumer (B2C) company. The more you're able to clearly define your target
customers, the more you will bring your executive
summary to life. Use examples of the types of companies
and people who will be your customer. For example,
Verizon would be a customer if you create components
for wireless broadband.

6. Achievements/Traction   Even if you are at the beginning of your journey, you must include any relevant
achievements on the part of you and your company. These

can include, but are not limited to, customers, orders, sales, recruitment of a management team or board, and the granting of a patent.

This sends the message to investors that you are serious about doing and are not simply in the business of coming up with ideas. This also has the benefit of adding credibility to the parts of your executive summary where you talk about the future.

7. Strategy, Tactics, and Execution   This is where you set out how and when you propose to achieve your business goals. Many businesses fail because the owner or team is unable to execute. Areas you want to consider addressing include: how you'll reach your target customers and persuade them to switch to your solution, what your distribution plans are, and how you will achieve and maintain an advantage over your competition.

8. Financial or Business Model   A common complaint made by investors is that executive summaries fail to include critical financial information. Investors understandably want to know what the potential return on their investment will be and within what time frame. You need to make clear how your business will generate revenue. Who will you charge what, and how often? Will you be using a "freemium" strategy initially and then introducing a premium paid service later on?

You should include a summary of financials including historical and projected revenue; earnings before interest, taxes, depreciation, and amortization (EBITDA); and important metrics such as volume. Although it's likely that investors will conclude that your projections are unrealistic, it's important to demonstrate that you understand and take the financial issues seriously.

9. Capital Requirements In this section you should include a summary of how much capital you have raised to date and how much you require in order to achieve specific milestones. Do not include a valuation in the executive summary. Valuations should not be included in the document but should be left for discussion.

10. Management Team At the end of your document, concisely list the founders and management team who are leading your business and their relevant experience and achievements. For many investors the team is one of the most important elements of a pitch, so although it comes at the end, it is one of the key sections in your executive summary.

There will no doubt be many things you will want to include in your executive summary, which could easily lengthen it to 6 to 10 pages. Resist the temptation to go beyond two to three pages; otherwise you increase the risk of your document being filed in the trash.

Remember, it is meant to be a *summary*. If there is additional information you would like the reader to have the option of reading, such as lengthy management bios, then include a link to the relevant page of your website. Finally, although many investors like the first document they read to be an executive summary, there is a growing trend on the part of investors to request sight of a pitch deck first. Ascertain their preference at the outset and then provide the information in the format they prefer.

The Pitch Deck

Most visual presentations are disasters. They are confusing, boring, uninspiring, and misused. The worst thing is that it isn't a secret. Death by PowerPoint is a syndrome as well known as many a medical condition. Despite the efforts of presentation design gurus such as Nancy Duarte (Slide:ology) and Garr Reynolds (Presentation Zen) to show the world a better way, by and large people continue to churn out the same text-laden pitch killers.

Adopt the following guidelines, and you will be streets ahead of the competition:

- *Make yourself the focus of your pitch rather than your visual presentation.* Your presentation is there to support and reinforce your key messages, not replace you.

- *Don't create a text-rich, picture-poor presentation.* People cannot read and listen at the same time. If your audience is reading from the text on your PowerPoint, they are not listening to you. The proper place for a text-rich document is either in the executive summary or presentation you send ahead or the document you leave behind.

    Do it like Steve Jobs, and use stunning visuals and the odd word or term here or there. Great visuals inspire and engage people emotionally. Of course there will be some slides where some text is necessary, but they should be the exception rather than the rule. If you must use text, try to follow Seth Godin's wise words of never more than six words on a slide.

- *Ban the bullets.* Bullets kill people, and bullet points kill presentations. Don't use them. They are unattractive and will detract from the aesthetic qualities of your images. If you heed the advice to abandon using text, then you will no longer have a need for them.

- *Don't use animations or transitions.* They are cheesy and overused, add nothing, and are distracting. Remember, you must remain the focus throughout your pitch.

- *Aim for simplicity and clarity.* Each slide should convey a single thought or idea.

- *Place your logo smartly.* Use your company logo on only the first and last slide so as to minimize any visual distractions.

- *Use quotes that support your key messages.* A slide with a single quote from a credible source can be very impactful.

- *Review and edit.* Once you have created your presentation, review it with the filter of asking whether or not each slide directly supports your primary objective, that is, securing investment or the sale. If it doesn't, delete it.

- *Address your audience's key concerns.* For an investor pitch, the topics that you cover will be the same as those identified for your executive summary earlier in this chapter and in Chapter 9.

Different Documents for Different Purposes

The form of the documentation that you provide to investors is important. At the outset, ascertain what the investor would like to see in advance of deciding whether or not to meet with you. Usually this will be either an executive summary or a pitch deck (usually PowerPoint).

Increasingly, investors, in particular venture capitalists (VCs), prefer to have a 10- to 15-slide pitch deck sent ahead that they can quickly thumb through. Ideally, this should not be the deck you use in your presentation. This is because the deck that you will use at your pitch should be text-light, visual-heavy (see Chapter 7). At your pitch, the role of your deck will be to support your presentation. You will verbally provide the details.

In contrast, when you send a deck ahead to investors, because you will not be there to provide the details, more textual information will clearly be required. Because it is still a deck rather than an executive summary, you should aim to convey the information as concisely and economically as possible. There will be some slides where only one or two words are necessary. Do not, in any event, go beyond four words by four lines.

Depending on what you have sent ahead, you should bring along two documents, a text-light deck to present with and a detailed text document to leave behind. Your presentation should never be your handout or leave-behind document. This is particularly important if the details of your pitch will be shared with other investors or partners who were not present at the meeting. You cannot rely on anyone else to communicate your pitch as well or as fully as you.

Adopting the approach advocated here requires you to abandon a traditional but ineffective way of presenting that will no doubt remain the status quo for some time. Fortunately, as an entrepreneur, you believe in innovation and doing things differently and better. Should you, however, need further persuading as to which approach is right, simply watch a Bill Gates presentation followed by a Steve Jobs one. Two great men, but only one delivers a great presentation and wows the audience.

Takeaways

- Keep your executive summary to two to three pages.
- Always aim for substance and style.
- Avoid Death by PowerPoint.
- Use minimal text with stunning visuals.
- Make yourself the focus, not your visual presentation.

Specific Audiences

9

The Sales Pitch

"You've got to start with the customer experience and work back toward the technology."

—Steve Jobs

Although most of the advice contained in this book applies equally to sales pitches as it does to investor pitches, there are specific issues that arise when pitching for new business that I'll address in this chapter.

For most entrepreneurs, the success of their business depends on their ability to secure new clients for their product or service.

Time and time again, start-ups with great products or services go out of business because their pitches fail to secure a sufficient number of customers to survive and grow. This chapter will show you how to develop contract-winning pitches and avoid deal-killing sales pitch mistakes.

It's About Them, Not You

One of the most frequently made mistakes during a sales pitch is when presenters focus on their companies rather than on the audience's problem and their solution. Companies will buy and hire your *solutions* to their problems, not your products and services.

The first minute of your pitch is critical. If your audience believes you understand their pain and can provide them with a solution, then you're more likely to gain and keep their attention than if you start by talking about yourself. So always begin by focusing on their problem and your solution, and make that the focus of your pitch.

An opening along the following lines will immediately get your audience's attention: "In this presentation, I am going to show you how you can reduce your distribution costs by 35 percents."

Steve Jobs, who, among his many other achievements, consistently delivered the best sales pitches the world has ever seen at the annual Macworld events, understood and demonstrated the importance of focusing on customer benefits of Apple's latest product. In a 2007 CNBC interview, Jobs was asked about the iPhone and its importance to Apple. Jobs answered, "We have the best iPod we've ever made fully integrated into it. And it has the Internet in your pocket with a real browser, real e-mail, and the best implementation of Google Maps on the planet. iPhone brings all this stuff in your pocket, and it's 10 times easier to use."

Although the reporter's question was about the importance of iPhone to Apple, Jobs focused on the benefits for Apple's customers.

Sales Pitch Structure

The following tried and tested formula will work for almost any sales pitch and is the most effective way of moving your audience to the action you want:

- Their problem
- Your solution
- Your team/company credentials
- Next steps

Let your audience know at the beginning of your pitch that this is the road map you intend to follow. People always like to be told what's coming.

Knowledge Equals Sales

If you're going to persuade your audience that you understand their issues, then you need to have done your homework. The greater your understanding of the specific challenges their business faces, the more equipped you are to customize your pitch for greater impact.

There are a number of ways you can increase your understanding of your prospects' problems. The easiest way is by picking up the phone and asking them about it. Ideally, you want to speak to one of the people you will be meeting, but there will normally be other people in the company who can help.

Use the Internet. If the company is big enough, then you should be able to find some useful coverage. Even if the information isn't directly on point, understanding the context in which the problem exists is helpful, as is understanding any other challenges the company is facing.

Many years ago, I was part of a start-up team pitching a large retailer with an innovative corporate responsibility (CR) solution. The retailer was already very active in supporting both social and environmental causes. Before the pitch we spent time trying to understand whether their current CR program had any obvious gaps that our solution could fill. During the course of our research we discovered a news article that mentioned that one of their new product lines was doing badly on the sales front.

Although this article was not about the company's CR program, the information enabled us to create a pitch that tied in our CR solution to their sales issue. At the beginning of our pitch, we signposted how we could address their CR needs and solve their sales problem at the same time. This unexpectedly resulted in the head of CR pausing the meeting and asking one of the key people in charge of product sales to join us. The outcome was that we ended up with a much bigger contract than we were originally pitching for.

As well as trying to understand as much as possible about the company you're pitching to, spend time research-ing the issues facing their sector. The more your prospect believes you understand about them and their challenges, the more they will want to do business with you.

Give Your Audience the Solution

Earlier, I talked about the importance of making your pitch problem- and solution-focused. It's one thing to tell your audience you have a solution that they can buy from you. It's another thing to give them something of real value before they pay you. Depending on what you're pitching, this may be useful advice, a plan, or a free trial of your product.

Software companies will typically offer customers a free day trial of their product, and consultants will often offer an initial free 20-minute consultation. Giving is a proven way of getting sales and should always be utilized in a sales pitch.

This approach has two benefits. First, if your advice, plan, or product proves useful, it will establish your credibility and the value of your product or service. Second, the desire to reciprocate is powerful. Give someone something of value, and that person will feel the need to give something back (hopefully a contract!).

Companies are used to being pitched with an *ask*, so it's always refreshing to be pitched with a no-strings *give*.

Think Conversation, Not Presentation

When I first started pitching Fortune 500 companies, the vice chairman of a leading investment bank, who was introducing us to a number of big retailers, said that whatever else we did in our pitch, we had to engage our audience in a conversation. Sound advice.

The last thing you want is an audience who sits quietly, waits until the end, and then says, "Thank you for your time, we'll be in touch." No, they won't.

A conversation enables people to connect and build a relationship. And as any savvy entrepreneur knows, relationships are a critical factor in any successful deal. So always seek to establish a *dialogue* rather than a *monologue*.

Sometimes a presenter will proceed as though their objective is to get through the end of their pitch in the fastest possible time, without being asked any questions.

Questions are a great opportunity to surface any unsaid concerns and allow you to address them, so encourage them.

James, a former client whose company had created a green heating system, recently contacted me after his sales pitch for a contract worth more than $100,000. He told me that his pitch had started out really badly because he arrived 30 minutes late due to a traffic accident, and to compound matters, his demo didn't work. He said by the time he had finished, he was sure his pitch had tanked.

Things turned around, however, when one of the executives James was pitching to asked him what he thought the impact of proposed environmental regulations would be on their current heating systems. James had researched this point ahead of the pitch and was able to immediately provide a comprehensive answer. This led to a discussion as to how his solution was compatible with the regulations, which resulted in the meeting carrying on for another 20 minutes.

James's company was ultimately awarded the contract. When we spoke, he said he was certain that but for that question it was all over. The question provided him with an opportunity to demonstrate his knowledge of the client's problem and his expertise and understanding of issues the industry was facing.

How to Encourage Questions

The most important key to getting your audience engaged is to make sure you're speaking to their issues and have a good, clear pitch style. Additionally, there are a number of effective techniques you can employ to encourage your audience to ask questions and engage with you.

First, make sure you pause between your key points. This allows the information to sink in and gives your audience a chance to reflect on any questions they may have. A pause of 2 to 3 seconds may seem long to you, but your audience will barely notice it. Pauses communicate confidence and self-control. Watch any clip of President Obama delivering a speech, and notice how he pauses between key points.

Second, leave sufficient time for a Q&A at the end of your pitch, and let your audience know that's the plan. If your meeting is an hour, make sure you leave at least 20 minutes for discussion. Whatever the length of the meeting, try to allocate one-third of that time for questions.

Third, ask your audience relevant questions. Obviously, you shouldn't ask questions where the answers are already in the public domain. That would suggest you hadn't done your homework. A well-thought-out question, however, can be a great way of starting a dialogue.

Bring Your Pitch to Life

I deal with this point more fully in Chapter 2. For maximum impact, your sales pitch needs to bring your product or service to life and inspire your audience to take action. This means using visuals such as PowerPoint or video and bringing along a demo or product samples.

The more you enable your audience to experience the benefits of your product or service, the easier it is to close the sale. Car salespeople understand this principle and will always encourage prospective buyers to sit inside the vehicle and take it for a test drive.

In *The Macintosh Way*, Guy Kawasaki endorses the use of demos in sale pitches as being a low-cost, effective way of outclassing your competitors' marketing and advertising. Kawasaki provides the following guideline for making a demo effective:

- Keep it short.
- Keep it simple and easy to follow.
- Make it "sweet." Show your hottest features.
- Make it fast-paced.
- Clearly demonstrate how your product offers a solution to a genuine problem your audience is facing.

If you have testimonials, bring along the actual letters or e-mails and hand copies to your audience. One former client would regularly take along video testimonials that he would show during his pitch. This is far more impactful than you simply telling your audience that you have testimonials. Whenever possible, you always want to *show* rather than *tell*.

Levers

Sometimes you may be pitching the solution that your prospect really needs at a price that is right, but for internal reasons that isn't enough to get them to move forward. This is particularly true of larger companies that often suffer from corporate inertia.

If this appears to be happening, then depending on the nature of your pitch, you should consider subtly sharing with them information that is likely to give them that extra nudge. Consider letting them know that there is a time limitation on what you're offering. This will only be effective if you are able to convince your audience that the reasons for the urgency are genuine.

Alternatively, if true, subtly let them know that you're talking to their competition. I was often amazed when pitching to companies how our audience became far more engaged the minute they realized we were talking to their competitors. At times it seemed as though getting an advantage over the competition was the most important factor.

Some words of caution: First, you should only consider using levers if they're true, not only because it's the right thing to do, but it's also sensible from a practical perspective. People speak to their competitors, and the last thing you want is to be exposed as dishonest at the beginning of your journey.

Second, if you decide to use levers, you must do so in a very subtle way. If it appears to your audience that you're providing information for the purpose of manipulating them into going with you, your pitch will fail.

And Now, a Few Words About You

Now although I've said that it's important that your sales pitch be problem- and solution-focused, you will still need to establish your credibility. Ideally, this should come toward the end of the pitch when you've got your audience hooked and told them what they want to hear.

Client testimonials can be very effective in reassuring your prospects that your company can and will deliver.

Use relevant success stories in your pitch to show how your solution has helped other companies. I talk about the importance and power of stories in Chapter 3. A success story that brings to life how your solution has helped another company can be one of the most potent moments of your pitch. People can begin to *see* how, if it worked for others, it can work for them.

Equally, if your company has won any awards or has any other notable achievements, such as board members who are highly respected in the industry, then mention them.

Finally, establish the credentials of the team behind the solution, talking about their qualifications and experience.

Takeaways

- Make sure the focus of your pitch is your audience's problem and your solution. Always remember, it's about them, not you.
- Give your audience something of value.
- Start a conversation rather than give them a presentation.
- Encourage questions to address unsaid concerns and to impress your audience with your expertise.

CHAPTER
10

The Investor Pitch

"If you can't explain it simply, you don't understand it well enough."

—Albert Einstein

The investor pitch is without doubt the toughest pitch you will ever have to deliver. It is not just the fact that the survival and future of your business may depend on the outcome of the pitch. It's also that you will be pitching to some of the smartest, most analytical minds on the planet, who in many cases are former entrepreneurs who have the insight to critically assess the claims and projections you make. These factors are compounded by the reality that many investors hear anything up to and beyond a hundred pitches a year and, consequently, have heard it all before.

Make no mistake, your chances of raising capital are very low if you can't pitch. Even if you have a business with great potential, the ability to pitch is nonnegotiable in the eyes of investors. From their perspective, if you can't deliver an effective, persuasive pitch, then how can you lead your company to success? How will you be able to raise further investment when it's needed or win big sales accounts?

Angel and Venture Capital Pitches

Although there are some minor distinctions between angel and venture capital (VC) pitches, this chapter focuses on the common features of both types of pitches. We have recently seen some of the traditional differences between angels and VCs begin to disappear with the emergence of "super angels" and "micro VCs." Super angels are investing in larger deals and micro VCs in smaller, early-stage deals.

A typical angel pitch will be for less than $1 million. Angel investors are usually well-connected, wealthy individuals who use their own money to invest. Angel pitches often last between 15 and 30 minutes and can be to an individual or group of angels. The angel(s) will sometimes decide at the first meeting whether or not to invest.

In contrast, a typical venture capital partnership:

- Will usually only be interested in investing a minimum of $2 to $3 million.
- Invests capital raised from institutional investors.
- Operates on the basis of broad partner consensus, although there will be a lead partner who promotes the deal.
- Conducts extensive due diligence.
- Will require governance and insist on board seats and complex deal terms, including the ability to influence later funding rounds.

A first meeting with a venture capital firm will normally be with only one partner but may just be with a principal or associate. It will last between 30 to 45 minutes and will often be a *screening* meeting. If it goes well, the entrepreneur will have the opportunity to pitch the partnership at a meeting that will last at least an hour.

Before the Pitch

There are a number of steps and decisions that you need to take beforehand that will have a bearing on the outcome of the pitch.

The Sweet Spot

Each investor and VC firm has its own favorite industry sectors, type, and stage of business that they prefer to invest in. This is known as their sweet spot. You need to make sure your business is aligned with the investor's sweet spot. In VC firms, each principal often has expertise in an even more narrowly defined subsector. If you're developing an enterprise software product and require $500,000, you should be targeting investors who have invested in the sector before at this investment level, not simply because they are more likely to be interested in investing, but also because they may have useful knowledge, experience, and connections that they can bring to the deal.

The Warm Introduction

Warm introductions will make it easier to meet with an investor, as well as make the pitching process smoother. Seasoned investors, in particular VCs, are difficult to access and reluctant to meet if you do not come via a trusted third party. If you are introduced to an investor by someone he or she knows and whose judgment is trusted, then the investor will have provisionally formed a favorable view of you.

This is not to say that the investor will invest in you simply because of the introduction, but it does make it easier to build a relationship, which, at the end of the day, is one of the most important factors in any decision to invest.

Notwithstanding the obvious benefits of securing a warm introduction, many entrepreneurs struggle to obtain one. Some investors view the ability to overcome this challenge as a measure of an entrepreneur's resourcefulness. If you cannot secure an introduction, then how will you manage to access potential client companies and journalists?

You can increase your chances of securing an introduction via a trusted third party in the following ways:

- *Always be networking.* Start doing this well before you need capital. It takes time to properly network and build relationships. It's a mistake, therefore, to start this process at the point when you need capital. Far better to have a conversation with an investor about what you're doing before you need capital. A foundation is then in place for approaching them down the line when you do need financing.

- *Use social media, in particular LinkedIn.* Many social media platforms enable members to identify friends and contacts of other members. This is useful for identifying your investor's network. LinkedIn has a useful facility that enables you to ask one of your contacts to introduce you to one of their contacts.

- *Talk to other entrepreneurs who have been funded by the investor you're targeting.* You may get some valuable insights into how best to pitch the investor, as well as an introduction.

- *Speak to corporate lawyers who work with entrepreneurs and investors.*

Nondisclosure Agreements

Entrepreneurs concerned about ensuring confidentiality will sometimes send or request an investor to sign a nondisclosure agreement (NDA). Don't waste your time. In a blog post entitled, "The Venture Capitalist Wishlist" Guy Kawasaki advises:

> Before you even start addressing the hard stuff, never ask a venture capitalist to sign a nondisclosure agreement (NDA). They never do. This is because at any given moment, they are looking at three or four similar deals. They're not about to create legal issues because they sign an NDA and then fund another, similar company—thereby making the paranoid entrepreneur believe the venture capitalist stole his idea. If you even ask them to sign one, you might as well tattoo "I'm clueless!" on your forehead.

If you feel strongly that your "secret sauce" (idea or proprietary technology) must be protected at all costs, then consider whether it's possible to pitch your concept without disclosing the information you want to protect.

Bear in mind, however, that this may get your relationship with an investor off to a bad start and begs the question whether you should be meeting with someone for the purposes of investing in your company if you don't trust that person.

Who to Bring to the Party

At a minimum the chief executive officer (CEO) of the company must always attend the pitch and should always do most of the presenting. If you are meeting a single angel or VC partner, then this may be sufficient and may make it easier for you to establish a one-to-one relationship with the particular investor.

If you go by yourself, make sure that you're ready to deal with all aspects of your business, from marketing to financials. It won't go down well halfway during the pitch to say, "I can't deal with the revenue projections because that's something my chief financial officer handles." As CEO of the business, investors expect you to have at least an overview of all key areas, especially the numbers.

If you are raising a large sum and are meeting with a group of angels or the VC partnership, bring along your key management team members. This is particularly important if they have responsibility for key "how and what" issues. Investors back teams first, ideas second. Bring only those members of your team who will be presenting, and make sure everyone is clear on both timing and their role during the pitch. Do not bring along junior or part-time staff.

The Content of Your Pitch

When you finally begin your pitch, you'll be providing information to your audience both verbally and visually through your presentation. You will also be providing information in response to questions. Key to delivering a winning investor pitch is making sure you address all of the important issues investors are concerned with. The more you can preempt your audience's questions, the more impressed they will be. There is no hard and fast rule as to structure; however, the following approach will go down well.

1. Open with an Overview As previously stated, it's important to open with a high-impact introduction. One of the best ways to achieve this is to provide your audience with a 90-second overview of the highlights of your pitch, in much the same way as a Hollywood trailer shows a preview ahead of a new release. You'll have to decide what are the strengths of your pitch, but you should in any event:

- Provide your name, role, relevant experience, and achievements. Investors are particularly interested in things you have already successfully built and launched. If you have members of your team with you, introduce them in the same way.
- Define what your company does in a single sentence.

- Explain what your core value proposition is.
- Explain your market size.
- Summarize traction such as customers, sales, grant of patent, and so on.
- Mention any awards, press coverage, or endorsements.

2. The Problem or Opportunity   Having wowed your audience with your opening, now you're ready to dive into the meat of your pitch by explaining the problem or opportunity. In most cases you will be highlighting an existing problem rather than looking at an opportunity where there is no real problem. An example of the latter is the iPod. No real problem existed, but Apple perceived an opportunity and created a demand. Very few companies achieve this.

The problem needs to be real and one you can objectively demonstrate. It should either be something that your audience will immediately recognize as a problem such as the relatively short life of laptop batteries. Alternatively, you must be able to establish that the problem exists by referencing credible independent research. Case studies can be helpful in bringing the problem to life, and graphics, such as a pie chart or graph, can be helpful in communicating the extent of the problem.

During an episode of ABC's TV show *Shark Tank*, one entrepreneur sought $100,000 for a 20 percent investment in her company that would create a sticky pad for sticky notes. The $10 pad would attach to the side of a laptop screen to hold the sticky notes in one central area.

The entrepreneur told the Sharks that people not having anywhere on their laptops to put their sticky notes was a genuine problem but did not, however, have any independent data to back this up. The Sharks quickly dismissed her pitch, rejecting her contention that there was a genuine problem.

Once you establish that there is a problem, you then have to show that the pain caused by the problem is sufficient to make people take action, that is, buy your solution. One way of doing this is by being able to show that people are currently paying other companies to solve the problem.

This leads to the final point that you need to address: how is the current problem solved, and why are these solutions inadequate? You need to convince your audience that you will either be able to reach a segment of the market that is not currently using existing solutions to solve the problem (perhaps because of cost) or that you will be able to persuade users of existing products or services to switch to your solution.

3. Your Solution   Having established that there is a genuine problem for which existing solutions are inadequate, you should then proceed to outline your solution. When you describe your product or service, don't make the mistake of focusing on its features. Your focus should be the benefit to consumers. Explain to your audience:

- *Whether you have a prototype.*
- *What your differentiator or competitive advantage is.* Demonstrate how your product is better than others already on the market. This is critical, particularly in a crowded market. Social networks are a great

example of a very crowded market coupled with a lack of differentiation. Despite the large sums raised by some of the most popular social networks such as Twitter, entrepreneurs rarely persuade investors to fund their new social network, often because they're unable to demonstrate differentiation.

- *How you will scale up.* Although both scalable and nonscalable businesses can be successful, only scalable businesses achieve the high-growth characteristics required to generate a return that's attractive to investors. The more scalable your business is, the more interest it will attract from investors.

- *Whether or not you have a patent or regulatory approval.* If you have copies of the patent or regulatory approval, bring them along to the meeting because you may be asked to show them to your audience.

A demo is a great way to bring your solution to life for the audience. Using a demo in your pitch also has the benefit of introducing a change to the format of the pitch, thereby keeping your audience's attention.

Although you can bring your demo to the meeting, you should consider presenting with a canned demo, that is, a video of your demo. You may want to do this when your demo is complex to demonstrate. This way you'll avoid the pain many entrepreneurs have endured of the demo not working during a pitch.

The best way to present your demo is to put yourself in the role of the person trying to solve the problem and walk your audience through how they will use your solution. Focus on the main use of the product rather than any secondary uses.

4. The Market   You may have an innovative product that addresses a genuine problem, but if you don't have a big market, investors won't be interested. The size of your market has a direct bearing on how much revenue your company can generate, so it must be properly addressed.

The common mistake that entrepreneurs make when talking about the market for their product is that they overstate the potential by talking in terms of the whole market rather than the total addressable market (TAM). Your TAM is defined by your specific industry and will be a subsegment of the market size. For example, within the automobile market, a subsegment would be convertibles or hybrids.

Let's suppose you created a new product for convertibles. If $100 billion is spent on automobiles each year and of that $3 billion is spent on convertibles, your TAM is potentially $3 billion rather than $100 billion. In fact, your TAM is likely to be even narrower depending on the cost of your convertible and other variables and the different subsegments that exist within the convertible market, for example, high-end versus popular. You should use graphics in your presentation such as a pie chart to illustrate the market and its segments.

Once you have defined your TAM, the next step is to address market growth. What is the current rate of market growth? What will the size of your market be in three and five years' time? A big market is essential; however, a big market with strong growth potential is compelling.

If there are any trends or megatrends that may have a bearing on your market growth such as aging populations or increased environmental regulation, explain their impact and relevance to your audience. Wherever possible, you should back your facts and figures up with credible research data such as Forrester or Gartner reports. These reports typically costs thousands of dollars, which presents a problem for many entrepreneurs. You can save money by looking at the press releases for the report produced by the company because these often contain the main findings. This will usually be sufficient for the purposes of your pitch.

5. The Competition   Your competitors are an asset to your pitch. Don't make the mistake of saying, "There is no competition" as some entrepreneurs do. When an investor hears this, they will conclude that this means either there's no demand or that the entrepreneur has not done their homework. Both conclusions will lead to the same negative decision.

You should present the topic of the competition in your visual presentation as either a competitive quadrant matrix or using a Harvey Balls slide. It's important to be realistic when dealing with the competition and to resist the temptation to show your competitor's product as having lots of weaknesses but your product having only strengths. Your competition is already in the marketplace and has customers. Investors like to see optimism in an entrepreneur but not at the price of realism.

Explain to your audience your strategy for getting your competitor's customers to switch to you. Is it easy for customers to switch to you, and what are the potential cost implications? And how will you defend against the established giants bringing better solutions into your market?

6. Sales and Marketing   If investors are satisfied that there is a problem and you have a solution and big market, their attention will turn to execution. A typical question from an investor will start with, "How will you?" As is so often said, lots of companies have great ideas, but few execute them well. Investors are very focused on ascertaining whether your company will be able to execute. Sales and marketing is all about execution, so you need to have your strategy buttoned-down tight for your pitch.

Your audience will want to know:

- What is your sales and distribution model?
- Who are your key target customers?
- How will you reach them? In other words, how will you raise awareness of your product or service?
- How many sales and marketing staff are required?
- What are your customer acquisition costs, and how long does it take to close a sale?
- Who will be your distribution channel partners?

7. Traction   Traction has always been an essential pitch ingredient. But in today's tough economic climate, being able to demonstrate traction is more important than ever and can often be the difference between yes and no.

The reason traction is so important to investors is because it typically demonstrates a shift from an idea to something that is on the path to being a profit-making business. Traction is progress and momentum.

There are many ways an entrepreneur can prove traction to an investor. Here are five of the most powerful:

1. *Get sales and customers.* This is one of the best ways of proving traction. Rather than spend endless months and years perfecting and refining your product, put your energies and creativity into snapping up paying customers.

2. *Recruit a strong management team.* A strong team is a huge asset. It provides reassurance to investors that you will be able to execute, and it also amounts to an endorsement of your business and you.

3. *Build an advisory board.* Sticking with the same theme, most start-ups would clearly benefit from having experts and gurus providing advice and general support. If you are able to engage some real names in your industry to act in an advisory board capacity, this will also provide some reassurance to investors.

4. *Secure strategic partners.* Whether it's a manufacturing, distribution, marketing, or media partnership, a strategic partnership is useful evidence of traction. A business that takes advantage of strategic partnerships can utilize the other company's strengths, which may make both companies stronger in the long run.

5. *Obtain a letter of intent (LOI).* It may be that your business is not yet ready to acquire paying customers.

The next best thing is an LOI from a large potential customer. The more LOIs, the better.

The more traction you are able to demonstrate to your audience, the closer you are to securing investment. If you pitch an investor without any traction, you run the risk of being told to come back when you have some.

8. Business Model and Financials   At the end of the day, investors are meeting with you to understand whether there is an exciting financial opportunity. They want to know how you will make money and how much money you will make. Although these elements may seem less exciting than your big idea, you have to deal with them thoroughly. Be prepared for your audience to challenge your financial assumptions and to expect you to be able to drill down on the details.

Although investors know that for an early stage company your revenue and profit forecasts are at best an educated guess, they still want to see the math behind your projections to both understand your revenue model and assess your ability to address the important financial issues.

In terms of your business model, you should explain how you will make money, addressing:

- Key elements including sales and distribution, direct and indirect sales, and your sales cycle.
- Whether it is a franchise, marketplace, listing fee, freemium model, or a combination.
- Key pricing metrics including users, account size, pricing, and lifetime.

In terms of financial projections, you should:

- Illustrate your three- to five-year revenue projections using charts. You should do this from the bottom up but validate from the top down.
- Explain the key assumptions behind your forecast.
- List the key drivers behind revenues and growth.
- Predict how long it will take to break even.

For many entrepreneurs, the financials are the most difficult aspect of the pitch to deal with. Although you should feel free to get help with building your financial model, you need to understand and be able to communicate its key pillars. Equally, although a chief financial officer (CFO) can deal with the details and any complexities at your pitch, investors will still expect you to be able to help them understand the fundamentals of your financial model. Simply handing over to your CFO is not likely to go down well, so take the time to educate yourself.

9. From Launch to Exit   It's important to show investors you have a road map and to share it with them. Ideally you want to map out the next five years for your company. As with the topic of financials, investors will understand that you are making an educated guess but will still want to know what your vision for the future is. You should therefore:

- Outline your five-year goals for the company.
- Set out your key milestones.
- Identify any major risks and challenges you face.
- Outline your thoughts on an exit strategy.

10. Funding Requirements   By now you will have whetted your audience's appetite with your exciting idea, impressive traction, and dazzling financial projections and are ready to move to the *ask*. This is the point at which you tell your audience how much you want and why. Tell your audience:

- Precisely how much investment you require.
- What the money will be spent on. You need to break this down to areas of your business such as staff or advertising.
- What your current burn rate is and what you expect your future burn rate to be.
- Whether you have had any previous investment and, if so, from whom. You should also let your audience know if you and any of your team have put money in. Investors like it when a founder has "skin in the game."
- What milestones will be achieved with the new funding.

Although valuation will be discussed, you should not deal with this in your pitch deck. This topic is best left for discussion.

11. End on a High Note   In the way that it's important you start strong, it's equally important that you end on a high note. An effective, memorable ending is to remind your audience of your three strongest points. For example, "In summary, product X is better than any similar product on the market, 150,000 customers agree with us, and we invite you to help us stay on course to reach our target of $3 million in sales next year."

Takeaways

- Target investors who are interested in your industry and sector.
- Seek out a warm introduction.
- Don't send an NDA.
- Use different pitch documents for different purposes.

11

Crowdfunding
Pitching to the People

"The crowd makes the ball game."
—Ty Cobb, American Major League Baseball Player

If you're raising funds for your start-up, you can't afford to ignore the crowdfunding revolution. Individuals, businesses, and nonprofits of all types are successfully using crowdfunding to fund part or all of their ventures, raising anything from several hundred to several hundred thousand dollars.

At its most basic level, crowdfunding involves the posting of a project on an online crowdfunding platform and asking family, friends, and members of the public to back it. You set a fund-raising target with a deadline by which the funds must be raised. Potential backers can then review your project and pitch and decide whether or not to support you.

There are thousands of crowdfunding success stories from all over the world and an ever-increasing number of crowdfunding platforms. The iPod Nano TikTok Watch Wrist Strap is probably one of the most well-known example of successful crowdfunding. Scott Wilson attempted to raise $15,000 on the popular crowdfunding platform Kickstarter to fund the production of two Nano watch kits. Scott exceeded his target and went on to raise an incredible $942,000 within three months without having to give away equity or take out loans.

Crowdfunding Historical Contribution

Crowdfunding is not a new phenomenon. The Statue of Liberty, a gift to the United States from the French in the late 1800s, almost failed to reach U.S. shores due to the American Committee's inability to raise sufficient funds to finance the site and the pedestal on which the statue would sit.

Joseph Pulitzer and his newspaper, the *New York World*, resorted to a form of crowdfunding and involved the American people in his campaign to complete the monumental project. His six-month crowdfunding campaign generated an awe-inspiring $100,000 in five short months through microdonations. Somewhat remarkably, more than 120,000 donations were less than a dollar.

And in the highest profile use of crowdfunding in recent times, President Barack Obama raised millions of dollars in the form of small donations from supporters via the Internet and viral marketing during his election campaign. At the time of this writing, President Obama has subsequently given his support for legislation that will relax tight regulations, thereby enabling equity-based crowdfunding to operate in the United States.

The Crowdfunding Pitch

As with the process of raising capital from investors, the creation of a compelling pitch is key to crowdfunding success. For the purposes of this chapter, I will use the term *pitch* broadly to include strategies and tactics that may also be defined as *marketing*.

The following differences are present between an investor and crowdfunding pitch:

- Crowdfunding involves pitching to the public rather than to a seasoned investor. This means a different approach to fund-raising is required to that delivered at a traditional investor pitch.

- It's more important that you are "likeable" in a crowdfunding pitch than that you have a good track record and relevant skills.

- You are not pitching in person but through your crowdfunding video and project profile. This, to some extent, limits your ability to make a connection with people and to establish a dialogue.

- On most crowdfunding platforms, you're not offering equity or a share of your profits to your backers but a reward instead. As mentioned previously, at the time of this writing, a bill with substantial bipartisan support that will relax the laws restricting equity-based crowdfunding in the United States was on its way to the Senate.

Selecting the Right Crowdfunding Platform

The number of crowdfunding platforms is growing every week. Although there is plenty of choice, it's critical to select a platform that's popular with your target market. If your project is in the creative realm, then Kickstarter and IndieGoGo are the two most popular platforms with the arts and film communities. Profounder is more focused on traditional entrepreneurial businesses, AppBackr is a platform solely for apps, and Crowdbackers focuses on projects by entrepreneurs and "geeks."

The Three Components of a Successful Crowdfunding Pitch

It isn't enough to have a great crowdfunding project and hope that people will back it. You can't just "build it, and they will come." This is a mistake that many people make with their crowdfunding projects and consequently they fail to achieve their funding goals.

Successfully promoting your crowdfunding project requires you to:

- Seed your project launch using established product-launch marketing strategies,
- Make sure your crowdfunding project page converts visitors to backers, and
- Promote and pitch during the period your project is live.

As can be seen, there are many parallels between promoting and pitching your crowdfunding project and launching and marketing a product.

Converting Visitors to Backers

A typical crowdfunding platform will allow you to post information about your project in the form of text, video, and images. These are your pitch assets, and this is where you make your pitch. People will back you because they like you and what you are doing, they like the rewards you're offering, or a combination of both. This means that in order to maximize your appeal, you need to make sure your crowdfunding pitch engages the different motivations people have for supporting a project.

Name and Description

As with any marketing activity, the name and description are critical to generating interest. You are competing for attention with hundreds of other crowdfunding projects, so invest the time to create an attention-grabbing name for your project and a persuasive project description.

Project Video

Your project video is your most important pitch asset and is a must if you're serious about getting your project funded. One crowdfunding platform recently reported that those projects that used video had a 125 percent better conversion rate than those that didn't.

Given people's short attention spans and lack of time, your video should be a maximum of 3 to 4 minutes. Ideally, you want to include both you and you product in your video. This is so that your audience can connect with you and also understand exactly what they're being asked to fund. Describing your product in words is not enough. Show them what it is and if it is functional, how it works.

The more professional your video, the more likely people are to believe that you will be able to deliver on your project if you receive the funding. By a professional video, I don't mean one that is loaded with special effects. That's easy to do. The key to a good video is the script. And the key to a good script is the story.

Inspire With Your Story

In Chapter 3, I explain the importance of stories to a traditional investor or sales pitch. The social nature of crowdfunding and lack of a physical pitch meeting makes it even more important that you include an inspirational story that is at the heart of your video and project text. This is important because, in most cases, people who back crowdfunding projects are not looking for a financial return.

Engaging people is the best way to persuade them to back your project, and a powerful, human story is the best way to engage people. So work out the elements of your story, and include them in your project profile and video. At a minimum, your story should explain who you are, what you hope to do, and why. If people like you are inspired by your story, they're more likely to back you.

Rewards

Most crowdfunding platforms allow you to offer a reward in return for financial backing. If you think in terms of your project page being your sales page, then you might view your rewards as the products your backers are pre-ordering. For those who are not your close family and friends, the rewards you offer will often be the biggest incentive to back you.

The following guidelines will help you get your reward strategy right:

- Offer a range of rewards for different levels of donation. The greater the donation, the better the reward.
- Make sure you factor in the total cost of providing the reward. For example, if shipping is required, what impact does that have on cost?
- Make the reward contingent on you getting the funding you require.
- Treat the reward as an opportunity to presell your product.

Get creative. Offer limited, premium versions of your products for those who make a sizeable donation. Provide your product to them before you make it available to the public. People like to be acknowledged, so look for ways that you can publicly give credit to those who support your project. Kris White offered those individuals who were willing to back his project to the tune of $1,000 the opportunity to have their likeness immortalized as a supporting character in his graphic novel *The 36*. Kris exceeded his fund-raising goal of $10,000 by eventually raising $11,474.

Be Transparent

Trust is at the heart of every crowdfunding relationship, given that your potential backers will almost certainly never meet or have a legally binding contract with you. It's therefore important that you are as transparent with your audience as possible. This includes spelling out exactly what you will use the funding for if you are successful. The more details you can provide, the more credible and trustworthy you will appear.

Prelaunch Pitching

Now that you have created your project page, let's look at what you should do by way of pitch preparation, before your project goes live. This is necessary because it's likely that your project will be open for a maximum of three months. It will take time to create awareness, so you want to avoid people finding out about it after your project has closed.

One of the keys to an effective prelaunch strategy is to let people know that something is coming. You need to create buzz and anticipation. There are various ways you can achieve this, including:

- Talking about what you are doing through Twitter, Facebook, or other social media posts. Casually let people know something's coming and that you're really excited about it. No hard sell!
- If you have a blog, writing a post about it.
- Building an e-mail list well ahead of your launch. You can do this by creating an opt-in e-mail on your website blog that provides people with something

valuable if they opt in, like a free report that gives useful information.

- Connecting between what you're offering people and the purposes of your crowdfunding project. This is to ensure that the people who are on your list are more likely to be interested in your project.

- Commenting on relevant blogs. A key to success for some crowdfunding projects has been being mentioned on relevant, popular blogs. You're in a better position to try to get exposure by the authors of popular blogs if you've already established a relationship with them and provided useful engagement.

- Creating a list of who your fans are, letting them know what you are doing, and asking for their support in promoting your project to their networks. If you have a start-up, then you need to be active on social media. If you are active on social media, then hopefully you have some close connections—let's call them fans for the moment—who will be happy to support your project by letting their networks know.

- Being an active supporter of other projects on your crowdfunding platform. Project owners will often reciprocate, so pay it forward.

Pitching When Your Project's Live

By now you have done your preparation, and you're ready to launch. From the moment your project goes live to the moment you close, you're in full pitch mode. Do the following to maximize your chances of crowdfunding success:

- *Leverage your close contacts.* Most people will be willing to help a family member or friend if asked. The problem is that most people don't ask, so they don't get. There are two things you can and should ask your close network for:

  a. to support your project.

  b. to let their networks know about your project.

  People need clear instruction, so tell them exactly what you need and want them to do. For example, give them a short description of your project and link to your project page so that they can share it with their networks.

- *Distribute your project video.* As soon as you launch, post your video on YouTube and other video-sharing sites such as Vimeo. TubeMogul provides a great free service that enables you to upload your video to a number of popular video-sharing sites in one action.

- *Ask popular bloggers and journalists to mention your project.* Create a short, clear e-mail explaining what you're doing, and ask them to check out your project. Only approach those who are likely to have any interest in your niche, and make sure you personalize each e-mail, perhaps letting them know you're a fan of their writing.

- *Use press releases.* Online news releases are an established way of raising awareness and getting links back to your site. Depending on your budget, you have the choice of free and paid news release services. Companies will frequently use this marketing strategy to promote the launch of a new product or service, and you should use it to promote your launch.

- *Leverage your social media network.* Everyone talks about social media marketing. This is because it's free and it works. The most popular networks are Facebook, Twitter, and LinkedIn, but you should post to any other networks that you're active on.

  Hopefully you have spent the time building your network up long before you launch. You want to make sure you are posting information about your project on a daily basis once you have launched.

  You don't want to bore or overwhelm your network with posts about your project, so try to stick to a ratio of no more than one project-related post for every four posts you make. And don't repeat the same post. Mix it up, make it interesting, and make sure you include a link to your project on all of your social network profiles.

- *Project page updates.* Most crowdfunding platforms allow you to provide project updates and communicate directly with your backers and supporters from your project dashboard. Make use of this facility. Continual engagement with your supporters can lead to them giving even greater support and is easier than trying to recruit new fans. Check out successful projects on the major crowdfunding platforms, and you'll see what I mean.

Note that you are likely to get most of your funding at the beginning and end of your project. This pattern is consistent with levels of sales during a traditional product launch.

The Future

Some people speculate that crowdfunding may one day replace traditional funding mechanisms. We are not there yet, but crowdfunding is certainly an option every business should consider even if only as a partial solution to funding requirements.

Although funding mechanisms may change, the ability to pitch will remain constant. The strategies and tactics I have outlined in this chapter have been utilized time and time again by the most successful crowdfunding projects in the world. Use them, and you'll dramatically increase your chances of crowdfunding success.

Takeaways

- Research the right crowdfunding platform.
- See your crowdfunding project launch.
- Leverage your network.
- Create a converting profile page.
- Offer desirable rewards.

12

Pitching the Media

"Without promotion something terrible happens . . . nothing!"
—P. T. Barnum, American Showman

For an entrepreneur, positive coverage in a national newspaper or leading blog can transform business. New customers, instant credibility, and becoming an overnight sensation are just some of the benefits that flow from being read at the right place and at the right time. And the best part for the cash-strapped entrepreneur is that there is no need to pay thousands of dollars to marketing and PR firms for this ultimate form of publicity. You just need to do the right things, in the right way, at the right time.

Why Most Entrepreneurs Fail to Get Media Coverage

A common approach adopted by entrepreneurs who are trying to secure media coverage is to do nothing until the point at which they want publicity. Then they compile a list of e-mail addresses for bloggers and journalists who seem to be in the right space and send one general e-mail that talks about their company and product or service and asks the journalist to write about it.

The problem with this approach is that it forgets that journalists and bloggers are people who see their role as providing useful and entertaining information to the public, rather than being there to provide publicity for entrepreneurs. The same advice that applies to pitching investors applies to pitching the media; namely, start building relationships before you need the publicity.

Think Laser Targeting, Not Mass Mail Out

Your first step should be to identify those newspapers, magazines, and blogs that you want coverage in. The key question here is who and what does your target market read? Getting covered in *Vanity Fair* may be great for your ego, but if your target market tends to read *TechCrunch* and *Wired*, then your efforts will reap very few rewards.

Once you have identified the blogs and print media that are relevant to your target market, you then need to add a dash of realism. Which on your list is most likely to be interested in covering a story relating to you and your company? If you're launching a new start-up and you have very little traction and don't have a big story, it will be much harder to be covered by the media with the largest readerships. So don't aim too high at the outset.

Once you have narrowed down your list to relevant media that are most likely to be interested, refine your list even further by identifying those bloggers and journalists who have covered similar issues and stories to yours in the past.

Building Relationships With Journalists and Bloggers

Now that you have your list of journalists and bloggers who you believe would be most likely to write something about you, the next step is to start building a relationship with them. The more you know about them and what they write about, the easier this is to achieve. So start reading their work and research them on social media.

When you come across something they have written that you think is a great piece, send an e-mail or post a comment on their blog. Maybe you have come across some new information relevant to a piece they wrote—in that case, share it with them.

A great way to start any relationship is to give rather than to ask. Journalists and bloggers need and welcome interesting issues and events that they can cover, so become a source of useful information, and establish a regular dialogue.

Transitioning to the Pitch

Once the relationship is in place (at least for a few weeks), then you can work on lining up your pitch. It's important that you tailor your pitch to the individual rather than adopting a one-size-fits-all approach. Send an individual e-mail that:

- *Is concise.* It should have no more than two to three paragraphs.
- *Has an attention-grabbing subject headline.* This is the best way to ensure your e-mail isn't deleted or ignored. The more you know about your target, the easier this will be to do. Something that intrigues the reader's attention and makes him or her want to read the rest of the e-mail can be very effective.
- *Pitches a story rather than a product or service.* The story you pitch will obviously mention your company

and product or service but should not be the central focus of the story. The stories most likely to be picked up are those that have a strong human element to them. Examples of stories that tend to get coverage are:

a. A new discovery story. This might be a revolutionary technology that will make people's lives easier or more enjoyable.

b. A story about one of your customers who was able to overcome a serious challenge using your product or service.

c. A success story. People love stories where individuals attain success against all the odds. If that's your story, pitch it.

d. A David and Goliath scenario. For example, you're the bootstrapping start-up that has launched a product that rivals those products in the markets that are made by established Goliath companies.

• *Is unique.* It's important that you see things from the potential reader's perspective because that is the filter that the journalist or blogger applies. Why does your story stand out, and what makes it a must-read?

Don't include attachments with your e-mail, but offer to provide more information if the journalist is interested, and make sure to include a link to your website. If you don't hear back within a few days, send a follow-up e-mail checking they received your first e-mail. Popular journalists are bombarded with pitches, so it may take time and persistence on your part before you get a result. It only takes one article about your company for your investment of time to pay dividends.

Some Useful Resources

Muck Rack (http://muckrack.com) monitors Twitter feeds from journalists. The journalists are organized by the subject matter they cover. Often, reporters will seek out sources through their tweets. If you respond immediately to their request for information, you stand a good chance of getting the journalist's attention.

HARO (Help a Reporter Out) (www.helpareporter .com) is a great place to list yourself as a source or expert for journalists. On a daily basis HARO e-mails a list of questions from reporters looking for immediate help with stories they are currently working on. You are able to select your area of expertise and ensure that you are only sent relevant queries.

Takeaways
- Build relationships with journalists first and early.
- Provide positive feedback and share useful content.
- Use laser targeting, not mass mail-outs.
- Pitch a story, not your company.

PART

IV

Preparation

13

Develop a Winning Mind-Set

"Eighty percent of success in a business is the psychology."
—Anthony Robbins

Confidence, vision, drive, and resilience are essential characteristics for every entrepreneur. When it comes to the pressure of a pitch, having a winning psychology is critical. This chapter will equip you with powerful techniques to eliminate any fears of pitching you may have and develop a laser focus.

Confidence

In the United States, public speaking is the number one fear. In the United Kingdom, it's the second most common fear.

Given what's at stake when you're pitching, it's easy to understand why so many entrepreneurs suffer from "pitch fright." Forgetting key information, being unable to speak coherently, and communicating fear are common symptoms.

Although a confident pitch won't get a weak business funding, a poor pitch will undersell a good business, losing the entrepreneur investment or new clients. Investors worry that an entrepreneur who can't pitch won't be able to bring on new investors and clients to grow their business. No matter how strong your start-up seems, you must be able to deliver a confident pitch.

The Myths and Science of Confidence

The term *confidence* comes from the Latin *confido* meaning "to have faith in." We recognize confidence the instant we see, hear, or meet it. Like charisma, it is a quality that people emanate and radiate.

There are many myths surrounding confidence, including that people either have it or they don't or that it takes years to develop. From my experience of having coached thousands of attorneys, judges, and entrepreneurs over many years, I know beyond a shadow of a doubt that people have absolute control over their confidence levels.

Scientific research from some of the leading research institutes in the world has consistently established that humans have the ability to radically and quickly change their emotions and self-perception using highly effective techniques based on recent developments from the fields of neuroscience, body language, neuro-linguistic programming (NLP), and psychology.

You can literally reprogram your brain with new beliefs about your abilities and supercharge your confidence levels to make sure you deliver a killer pitch. And the best part is that this transformation can be achieved in hours and days, rather than months and years.

To reap these rewards, there is one requirement. Read this chapter, and do the exercises. As the ancient Chinese proverb from Confucius who wisely observes:

"I hear, I forget.

"I see, I remember.

"I do, I understand."

The Power of Belief

"One person with a belief is equal to a force of 99 who only have interests."

—John Stuart

The power of belief should never be understated. People change history because of the power of their beliefs. Whether it is starting a war, going to the moon, or recovering from a terminal illness, belief is one of the most powerful resources a person has.

Beliefs affect how you feel and act. People will often fail to try something because they *believe* they will not succeed. Equally, they may try but not believe and consequently fail. Belief is therefore at the core of confidence, which is why people will often describe someone who lacks confidence as lacking in self-belief.

Until 1954 it was widely believed that it was not possible for humans to run a mile in less than 4 minutes. That was the year Roger Bannister shattered that belief, by doing exactly that. Bannister said that it was in his mind that he really made the achievement—he ran the 4-minute mile so many times in his imagination that he made it a belief that became an achievement.

People have a tremendous ability to instantly change their beliefs, behavioral patterns, and actions. But human nature is such that people often only change when they have a really good reason to do so, when in their minds they have sufficient leverage to do what is necessary.

We have heard of stories of mothers demonstrating superhuman feats of strength and courage when their children are in danger. People will do the impossible when they believe that the pain of not taking action would be far greater than the pain of not doing the thing you have always been scared of. You need to ensure, therefore, that you have empowering beliefs if you are to maximize the effectiveness of your pitch.

Identity

Closely linked to belief is the concept of identity. Like beliefs, events and other people shape our identity. Entrepreneurs who fail with their first start-up may choose to define themselves as a failure. Equally, entrepreneurs who have negative pitch experiences may consequently define themselves as people who just can't pitch.

Once you define yourself this way, you increase the chances of failing time and time again. It's the beginning of a slippery slope. You'll continue to act in a way that reinforces this negative identity because people have an internal need to act consistently with how they define themselves. People will often say, "I would never do that. I am not that kind of person." This belief of identity becomes a self-fulfilling prophecy. *I think I am; therefore I do; therefore I am.*

If a person believes he or she is a great pitcher, that person will try to secure as many pitch opportunities as possible, look forward to them, and pitch with confidence. Conversely, an entrepreneur who lacks confidence in his or her pitching skills will not be so keen to line up pitches and, when opportunities do come along, will usually pitch badly.

"I think, therefore I am."

—*Descartes*

Discarding Your Limiting Beliefs

The first step in creating a winning mind-set is to delete your limiting beliefs. The following two tried and trusted processes will help you do this.

Step 1: Face the Consequences

Write down all the consequences that you have suffered, are suffering, and will continue to suffer because of your belief that you pitch badly. Think carefully about the lost opportunities resulting from this belief.

Write down as many negative consequences that you can think of, and try to emotionally connect with what this will mean for your ability to succeed with your business and life. By linking pain and suffering to your limiting beliefs, you give yourself leverage to change and abandon your old limiting beliefs. Whenever you start to think you can't pitch, reread your list.

Step 2: Devil's Advocate

Now it's time to start chipping away at your disempowering beliefs. Write down on a single piece of paper all of the reasons that your limiting beliefs are wrong. For example, if you believe you are unable to pitch, you might write down the fact that many other entrepreneurs have overcome this common belief and gone on to raise capital.

Get creative, and work hard to show why your beliefs are wrong. Lawyers are not the only ones who can find two or more interpretations to a situation. By engaging in this process, you begin to cast doubt on what may have been firmly held, albeit wrong, beliefs. Again, if the self-doubt starts to return, remind yourself why it is wrong.

You now have all of the reasons and leverage you need to discard your old beliefs. Both consciously and unconsciously, you are connected to their cost.

Step 3: Visualization

Now that you have taken the first steps toward destroying your limiting beliefs, you can start the process of replacing them with new empowering beliefs.

Visualization is without doubt one of the most effective human performance tools of our time. Backed by neuroscience and supported by research from leading universities, visualization is a thoroughly researched human performance technique based on scientific principles and an understanding of the human brain. When practiced correctly, it can transform your ability to pitch.

Visualization has long been used successfully by Olympians and other professional athletes such as Jack Nicklaus, Tiger Woods, and Michael Jordan to improve their performance. Former world champion bodybuilder,

Hollywood superstar, and former governor of California, Arnold Schwarzenegger, well known for his use of visualization, once said,

> When I was very young I visualized myself being and having what it was I wanted. Mentally I never had any doubts about it. The mind is really so incredible. Before I won my first Mr. Universe title, I walked around the tournament like I owned it. The title was already mine. I had won it so many times in my mind that there was no doubt I would win it. Then when I moved on to the movies, the same thing. I visualized myself being a famous actor and earning big money. I could feel and taste success. I just knew it would all happen.

Many other successful superstars, including Donald Trump and Oprah Winfrey, have used visualization to help them achieve their goals. It has worked for people the world over, from every walk of life, and can absolutely help you deliver a great pitch.

It's a fact that we tend to get what we focus on. When you consistently visualize something, you bring about physical changes to your brain, creating new neural networks that enable you to achieve your goals faster and more effectively. Visualization engages your creative powers and reticular activation system (RAS) to look for solutions and resources to ensure that you achieve your goal in the quickest time possible.

The principal reason visualization is so effective is because the primal part of the brain that governs our fear response cannot tell the difference between an actual experience and the future memories you vividly imagine.

The more you can clearly visualize something, the more focused you become and the more likely you will do it well. When you start to create positive future memories of yourself pitching through the correct visualization process, not only will you achieve your desired outcome but you will also find that negative past memories lose their power over how you feel and what you achieve.

There is a great deal of misunderstanding about the process of visualization. You cannot simply imagine what you want and wait for it to happen. To gain the benefits, you must take the following specific steps:

Visualization Technique

- Set aside 5 to 10 minutes first thing in the morning and last thing at night. This technique is more effective if you can practice it twice a day. As with your muscles, the more you do it, the more you will build and strengthen your new neural networks, which in turn will help ensure you achieve your desired outcome.

- Ensure you are in a good emotional state. If you are not, try playing one of your favorite music tracks or remembering and focusing on a very positive memory.

- Decide on something *specific* you want to achieve such as delivering a knockout pitch at your meeting next week.

- Visualize yourself having achieved those things, in other words, *as having achieved your desired goals*.

- Make your visualization as detail rich as possible. See the clothes you're wearing when you pitch, and hear the words you're saying. The more detailed you can make the visualization, the more effective the process.

- Experience the emotions you will feel when you deliver a successful pitch and achieve your desired outcome. Make the emotions as intense as possible, and enjoy the moment.

- Alternate between visualizing through your eyes and seeing what is going on around you and watching yourself as though on film. See what approach works best for you, and stick with it.

- Replay the visualization again, but this time with even more intensity and detail.

Some people maintain they cannot visualize. They're wrong. If you can close your eyes and remember what your spouse or car looks like, then you can visualize. It's true that some people find it easier to see the images with detail and clarity than others; however, as with all things in life, consistent practice will lead to improvement. If you really can't see the image in detail, the technique will still work if you simply think the thought without the picture.

Repeat this process twice daily for a week, and you will soon begin to experience the changes within you. Make this part of your daily routine, and you will be well on your way to making your vision a reality. And remember, by using visualization, you are in the company of the most successful people on the planet.

As Roman Emperor Marcus Aurelius once said, "Our life is what our thoughts make it."

Takeaways

- You control your confidence levels.
- Destroy and discard your limiting beliefs.
- Use visualization to create a successful future.

14

Prepare to Win

"By failing to prepare, you are preparing to fail."
—Benjamin Franklin

Three undisputed truths:

- Delivering a winning pitch will often determine the survival and success of a business.
- People create their best work when they have time, space, and silence.
- Proper rehearsal is critical to delivering a professional, persuasive performance.

Despite these truths, most pitch preparation takes place at the eleventh hour, amid constant distraction and noise with minimal, if any, rehearsal. Small wonder that most pitches are weak and ineffective and so fail.

Time

"The first draft of anything is shit."

—Ernest Hemingway

There are two phases to all pitch preparation. The first is the creative process where you create your presentation and prepare your delivery. The second phase is rehearsal. Both take a considerable investment of time—days, weeks, and months, rather than seconds, minutes, and hours.

The greatest performers, athletes, and world-class experts from every field are not "naturals." They reached the top of their game through using effective techniques and investing thousands of hours in preparation.

Neuroscientist Daniel Levitin, in *This is Your Brain on Music*, talks about 10,000 hours of practice being the magic number to achieve mastery:

> . . . ten thousand hours of practice [are] required to achieve the level of mastery associated with being a world-class expert—in anything. In study after study, of composers, basketball players, fiction writers, ice skaters, concert pianists, chess players, master criminals, and what have you, this number comes up again and again. Ten thousand hours [are] the equivalent to roughly three hours per day, or twenty hours per week, of practice over 10 years. . . . But no one has yet found a case in which true world-class expertise was accomplished in less time. It seems that it takes the brain this long to assimilate all that it needs to know to achieve true mastery.

Steve Jobs, wrongly perceived by many to be a naturally gifted performer, was reported in *Businessweek* to spend "grueling hours of practice" when preparing his Macworld keynote speeches, a process Jobs began weeks ahead, even though he had been delivering spectacular keynote speeches for years. Jobs made presenting look easy because he worked so hard at it.

This triumph of time and practice over the notion of *natural* world-class performers was considered by K. Anders Ericsson, a Swedish psychologist, Conradi

Eminent Scholar and professor of psychology at Florida State University. Ericsson, who is widely recognized as one of the world's leading researchers on expertise and has studied world-class achievers from every walk of life, concludes in "The Making of an Expert" *(Harvard Business Review)*, that outstanding performance is the product of years of deliberate practice and coaching, not of any innate talent or skill. According to Ericsson:

> To people who have never reached a national or international level of competition, it may appear that excellence is simply the result of practicing daily for years or even decades. However, living in a cave does not make you a geologist. Not all practice makes perfect. You need a particular kind of practice—deliberate practice—to develop expertise. When most people practice, they focus on the things they already know how to do. Deliberate practice is different. It entails considerable, specific, and sustained efforts to do something you can't do well—or even at all. Research across domains shows that it is only by working at what you can't do that you turn into the expert you want to become.

Starting your preparation well in advance of a pitch allows you time to research, reflect, and revise. Time gives you the opportunity to step back and look at the big picture and develop and refine your pitch so that you avoid the pitfall that Hemingway highlights in the quote at the beginning of this chapter.

Your choice is simple. If you want to create a forgettable, boring pitch that fails, simply spend a few hours at the last minute rehashing a pitch you delivered previously. If, however, you want to create a pitch that motivates your audience to take action, start your preparation weeks in advance of your meeting, and be prepared to invest days, if not weeks, in its creation.

Peace

"Others inspire us, information feeds us, practice improves our performance, but we need quiet time to figure things out, to emerge with new discoveries, to unearth original answers."
—Ester Buchholz, Psychoanalyst
and Clinical Psychologist

Producing a pitch that excites and inspires is a creative process. Creativity needs peace and quiet to flourish. Uninterrupted thought is a precondition that necessitates time away from the laptop, smartphone, office, or other distractions. Unfortunately, along with not taking the time to prepare a great pitch, people rarely allow themselves the necessary space, peace, and quiet.

Research confirms that a steady stream of incoming information is one of the best ways to destroy creative thought and clarity. A study commissioned by Hewlett-Packard found that frequent use of e-mails and text messages has a detrimental effect on the brain and a noticeable drop in IQ, equivalent to smoking two joints of marijuana.

Our increasing obsession with being always available and connected comes at the high price of creativity and clarity. This obsession also impacts the attention given by pitch audiences. Entrepreneurs who have pitched a group of investors will frequently report that one or more investors seemed to spend much of the meeting using their smartphones. This attention deficit problem simply reinforces the need to make sure your pitch contains a compelling story that cuts through the noise.

If your pitch is a priority, start the creation process in a place that you cannot be disturbed or distracted. Turn all phones off, and shut down your e-mail. Ideally be somewhere peaceful, away from your office or work space so that the *residue* or reminder of noise and distraction does not impinge on your creativity. Then begin.

Brainstorm

Having set aside the time and established the optimum conditions for creating and preparing your pitch, you can now begin the first step—the brainstorm. Brainstorming is more effective when done with sticky notes and a whiteboard rather than a computer presentation program. This is particularly so when you are brainstorming as part of a team. The reason for this is that brainstorming is a means to an end, whereas PowerPoint and Keynote are an end in themselves.

Start by defining the important questions you need to answer. These will often include:

What is my single overriding objective?

Who is my audience?

What do they want to see and hear?

What is the one message I want them to take away
and remember?

What is the pitch story?

Once you have defined your questions, now begin to
answer them with both facts and ideas. At this stage, do
not filter. If something seems to have a connection, however tenuous, then write it on a sticky note or the whiteboard. Brainstorming is a right-brain creative process,
and something useful may be suggested by the right brain
that the logical left brain does not immediately recognize.
When organizing brainstorming sessions, I try to make
the environment and circumstances as supportive as possible such as organizing plenty of refreshments and food.

Once you have completed your brainstorming session, step away, forget about it, and do something else.
This allows for the regaining of perspective and for the
brain to ponder in the background on the ideas that have
been generated.

Distill

Now you need to distill the ideas and facts you have
generated. Decide which ideas and facts support your
primary objective, help answer your key questions, provide
context, and then discard the rest. You need to be brutal
in this process. Apply the test of "So what?" to each piece
of information. If it isn't immediately obvious how it
bears on your primary objective, then it probably isn't
relevant.

Research

Now that you have identified the facts and figures you wish to use in your pitch, treat them as items requiring further investigation. It's important that any facts and figures you propose to rely on in your pitch are accurate, current, and in some cases sourced. Sourcing is particularly important when you are talking about topics such as the extent of a problem your company solves and market size. You will also find that this process of investigation and validation brings other relevant facts to your attention that you may not have been aware of.

Bearing in mind that your pitch is as much about *them* as it is about you, it's important that you research your audience. The more you know about whom you're pitching to, for example, their values, interests, past investments, and so on, the more you can tailor your pitch and infuse it with areas of common ground and relevance.

Structure

The next step is to give your ideas and facts some structure. Structure ties the pieces of information together and helps the audience make sense of your pitch. A pitch that wanders without any apparent logic or familiar path will lose attention and cause confusion.

Depending on the type of pitch you are preparing for, you may want to use a chronological, features-and-benefits, opportunity, or problem/solution structure. Although there are other structures or flows that can be used, these four are the most popular and will work for most pitches.

A chronological structure usually organizes the information and ideas according to the time that the events occurred. A features-and-benefits structure is often used in a sales context. You would talk through the features of your product and then outline the benefits for your prospective customer.

An opportunity structure is organized around a new opportunity that you wish to take advantage of or are offering your audience. And last, a problem/solution structure is the classic form adopted in an investor pitch. The entrepreneur has identified a problem and seeks investment to develop, launch, or market the solution.

Script

In Chapter 8, I discussed the importance of your delivery being the focus of your pitch with your visual presentation playing a supporting role of reinforcing your key messages. With this in mind, the next step of the process is to create the script *or* outline of what you will say.

You have decided on the ideas and facts you will use and have created the structure to insert them. Now you create the thread that connects them together and enables your audience to understand and remember your pitch.

I have referred to the creation of a script or outline. This is because some people prefer to write their pitch out in full, whereas others prefer to create an outline with summary notes for each topic. After more than 20 years of delivering speeches and pitches, where lives or millions of dollars have been at stake, I have found the following hybrid approach to be the most effective.

- Write out your pitch in full. It is only when you complete this process that you can truly know what you are going to say and how long it will last.

- Practice delivering your speech until you can say it back to front, while standing on your head, without reading from your script. I talk more about the rehearsal process next. It's important to note that you should not attempt to memorize your speech because it will lead to your delivery sounding lifeless and canned.

- Edit your speech according to the feedback you receive and the views that you form during rehearsal.

- At this point, depending on your level of confidence and ability to deliver your pitch without reading from the script, either:

  a. Determine to deliver your pitch without any notes or prompts. The upside to this approach is that it enables you to be far more engaging, to focus on your audience, and to be perceived as more impressive. The risk is that you lose your thread or go off on a tangent. Or

  b. Use the notes facility in PowerPoint or Keynote's presenter notes for providing triggers and signposts that help keep you on track.

As I explained in Chapter 8, your visual presentation should have minimal, if any, text, which means you cannot and should not be reading from it. Adopting the approach just mentioned will enable you to deliver a professional, persuasive pitch whether you know your material and pitch inside out or are less familiar with it.

Customize

In Chapter 2, we looked at the importance of establishing a connection with our audience. By adopting the common practice of simply reusing the same pitch and visual presentation time after time, you lose a valuable opportunity to connect. Customize your pitch as much as possible so that it speaks to your audience's values, issues, and concerns. This will ensure that your delivery sounds fresh and assure your audience that they are not just *another* potential investor or client.

This means more than simply adding their logo to your presentation. You can customize your pitch by:

- Referring to both the names of individual members of the audience and their company throughout your pitch. People love the sound of their own names.
- Referring to a current event, ideally something that has happened on the day of your pitch or just before.
- Mentioning something that is local to your audience.
- Tying your product or service into something that belongs to your audience such as showing how your solution can address its specific problem.

Rehearse

Although you may not have Levitin's 10,000 hours to prepare and rehearse your pitch or even the time that Jobs put into his keynote presentations, full rehearsals are a critical step on the path to persuasion. Put simply, the more you rehearse your pitch, the more confident you feel and the more effective your delivery.

Although this may seem obvious, very few people preparing for a pitch or presentation take the time to do even a single full rehearsal. Clients frequently say to me that they intend to give their pitch a quick run-through on the morning of the pitch. Rehearsing with a quick run-through is the route to a quick "No thank you."

A full rehearsal is where you (and your team, if participating) deliver every word of your pitch aloud along with the visual presentation that you will use. The more you replicate the likely conditions of your pitch, the more effective the process. For example, if you'll be standing during your pitch, then stand during your rehearsal. Ask colleagues and friends to be your audience. This not only makes the pitch rehearsal more realistic but also provides you with people who can supply constructive feedback.

To start out with, you will need to read from your script. Time your rehearsals so that everyone knows when he or she is up to speak and so that you stick to the time limit you have agreed on with your audience.

You should also rehearse answering questions that you anticipate being asked. Prime your rehearsal audience with the questions, and decide who will be answering what questions. Nothing should be left to chance. Although the first part of your pitch preparation was a creative process, your rehearsal and pitch must be planned and run like a military operation.

In addition to receiving feedback from your audience, you should also record your pitch rehearsal. Many people are uncomfortable seeing themselves perform on camera. It is, however, far better that you see your mistakes before your real audience does. When playing back the video, focus on your body language, as well as your vocal delivery. In particular, watch out for "ums" and "ahs," which many accomplished performers, including President Obama, fall victim to.

In terms of how many rehearsals are necessary, there is no maximum. The more you rehearse, the better you will perform and the more confident you will become. The real question is not, "How many rehearsals should you do?" but rather "How good do you want to be?" In terms of a minimum number of full rehearsals, five seems to be right for most people. Any rehearsal, however, is better than no rehearsal.

Takeaways

- Preparation takes time, so make some time to prepare.
- Prepare with peace and quiet.
- The more you rehearse, the better you will perform.

Bibliography

Introduction

Bussgang, J. "Being the 1 in 300." Chapter 3 in *Mastering the VC Game*. 2010. p. 77.

Garber, A. "Death by PowerPoint." *SmallBusinessComputing.com*, April 1, 2001, www.smallbusinesscomputing.com/biztools/article .php/684871/Death-By-Powerpoint.htm.

U.S. Small Business Association (SBA), "Frequently Asked Questions: Advocacy Small Business Statistics and Research," http://web.sba.gov/faqs/faqIndexAll.cfm?areaid=24.

Chapter 1

Cialdini, R. *Influence: The Psychology of Persuasion* (New York: Harper Paperbacks, 2006).

Hart, L. *How the Brain Works: A New Understanding of Human Learning, Emotion, and Thinking* (New York: Basic Books, 1975).

Haynes, J. D. "Decoding Mental States From Brain Activity in Humans." *Nature Reviews Neuroscience* 7 (July 2006) 523–534.

Shinn, F. *The Game of Life and How to Play It* (Los Angeles, CA: DeVorss & Company, 1978).

Wilson, T. D. *Strangers to Ourselves: Discovering the Adaptive Unconscious* (Cambridge, MA: Belknap Press, 2004).

Chapter 2

Goode, M. R., Dahl, D. W., and Moreau, C. P. (2010). *The effect of experiential analogies on consumer perceptions and attitudes. Journal of Marketing Research, 47, 274–286.*

Medina, J. *Brain Rules: 12 Principles for Surviving and Thriving at Work, Home, and School* (Seattle, WA 2009).

Mehrabian, A. *Silent Messages: Implicit Communication of Emotions and Attitudes* (Stamford, CT: Wadsworth Publishing Company, 1972).

McNeill, D. *Gesture and Thought* (Chicago: University of Chicago Press, 2007).

Chapter 3

Gasset, J. O. *The Dehumanization of Art and Ideas About the Novel* (Princeton, NJ: Princeton University Press, 1948).

Chapter 7

Duarte, N. *Slide:ology* (Sebastopol, CA: O'Reilly Media, 2008).

Reynolds, G. *Presentation Zen: Simple Ideas on Presentation Design and Delivery* (Berkeley, CA: New Riders Press, 2008).

Chapter 13

Ericsson, K. A. "The Making of an Expert." *Harvard Business Review* (July 2007).

Levitin, D. *This Is Your Brain on Music: The Science of a Human Obsession* (New York: Plume/Penguin, 2007).

TNS Research. "E-mails 'Hurt IQ More Than Pot,'" April 22, 2005, http://edition.cnn.com/2005/WORLD/europe/04/22/text.iq.

Index

market, focus on
  in elevator pitches, 71
  in executive summary content,
    97–98
  TAM (total addressable
    market), 71, 98, 131
  in venture capital pitches,
    131–132
McNeill, David, 21, 22
media, pitching to, 157–159
media coverage
  importance of, 155
  lack of for entrepreneurs,
    155–156
  targets for, identifying, 156
Medina, John, 30, 33
Mehrabian, Albert, 20, 23
memorable moments, 33–35
memory, stories and, 40
metaphors, using, 45
Mies, Ludwig, 91
mind-sets, winning. *See*
    confidence; pitching to
    win techniques
Mohammed (prophet), 45
Monroe, Marilyn, 33
Muck Rack, 159

N
names, importance of, 145–146
National Entrepreneurs'
    Day, xiii
Nature Neuroscience, 6
neediness, avoiding, 9–12
nerves, speech and, 24–25

networking, 124–125
  See also social media
neuro-linguistic programming
    (NLP), 55, 166
neuroscience
  adaptive unconscious, 6
  on average attention spans, 30
  on confidence, 166
  reactance theory, 10
  reptilian brain, decision
    making and, 6–9, 10, 16
  on time needed for
    practice, 178
new media. *See* e-pitches; social
    media
news releases, 150–151
Nicklaus, Jack, 170
nondisclosure agreements
    (NDAs), 125–126
nonverbal communication,
    20–23

O
Obama, Barack
  on confidence, 14
  crowdfunding, use of, 142
  on entrepreneurship, xiii
  metaphors, use of, 45
  pauses, use of, 25, 115
  "thinking in threes," use of, 35
  "ums" and "ahs," use of, 188
openings, pitch. *See* content
    guidelines; introductions
open posture, 22
Oprah, 19, 23, 171

3/14/12